PART-TIME REAL ESTATE INVESTING FOR FULL-TIME PROFESSIONALS

Upgrade your mindset, portfolio, and finances in less than a year while working

DEREK M. CLIFFORD

Part-Time Real Estate Investing for Full-Time Professionals
Copyright © 2020 by Derek M Clifford.

All rights reserved. No part of this publication may be reproduced, distributed or transmitted in any form or by any means, including photocopying, recording, or other electronic or mechanical methods, without the prior written permission of the publisher, except in the case of brief quotations embodied in critical reviews and certain other noncommercial uses permitted by copyright law.

Although the author and publisher have made every effort to ensure that the information in this book was correct at press time, the author and publisher do not assume and hereby disclaim any liability to any party for any loss, damage, or disruption caused by errors or omissions, whether such errors or omissions result from negligence, accident, or any other cause.

Adherence to all applicable laws and regulations, including international, federal, state and local governing professional licensing, business practices, advertising, and all other aspects of doing business in the US, Canada or any other jurisdiction is the sole responsibility of the reader and consumer.

Neither the author nor the publisher assumes any responsibility or liability whatsoever on behalf of the consumer or reader of this material. Any perceived slight of any individual or organization is purely unintentional.

The resources in this book are provided for informational purposes only and should not be used to replace the specialized training and professional judgment of a health care or mental health care professional.

Neither the author nor the publisher can be held responsible for the use of the information provided within this book. Please always consult a trained professional before making any decision regarding treatment of yourself or others.

Cover Design by 100Covers.com
Interior Design by FormattedBooks.com

ISBN: 978-1-7348932-0-5

FREE GIFT!

Thank you for purchasing this book! In order to set you up and keep you going in the right direction, check out a few free gifts from me to you!

At the link below, you'll find out which type of investment vehicle may be best for you!

http://elevateequity.org/which-investing-type-is-for-me-quiz

Additional bonus: after finding out which type of investing is right for you, receive a copy of my Elevate Your Equity Step-By-Step Plan, which will help guide you through the investing process and outline everything you need from A-to-Z to getting your first chunk of rental equity out of state, whether its single family or multifamily.

DEDICATION

For my wife, Sophie.

For pushing me farther than I thought possible.

For her patience, support, understanding and strength.

For showing me how a balanced inner world manifests outward, into the real world and inspires everyone.

"Don't wish it was easier, wish you were better. Don't wish for less problems, wish for more skills. Don't wish for less challenges, wish for more wisdom.

—Jim Rohn

CONTENTS

Introduction: Dare to Question Your Reality XIII

Chapter 1: LEGO Blocks and My Story 1
    Preparation & Self Gratification 2
    Taking the Plunge 3
    Hey, Maybe This Isn't So Bad 3
    Expansion & Bigger Plans 4
    What's in Our Near Future Together 5

Chapter 2: Advantages of Real Estate as an Investment 9
    What's So Great About Real Estate? 10
        Outlook 13
        Reliable Demand 14
        Options 14
        Acquisition 14
        1031 Exchanges 16
        Tax Advantages 17
        Business Status 17
        Passive Income 18
        Hedge on Inflation 19
        Outperform Any Other Asset Class 22
    Appreciation 23
    Equity Capture 24

Depreciation 25
Cash Flow 27
Debt Paydown 27
Providing A Home for A Family That Needs It 29
Intangible Benefits of Investing in Real Estate 30

Chapter 3: Disadvantages of Real Estate Investments 35
Responsibility 36
Illiquidity / Loss of Direct Control 37
Rehab Budget Overruns or Trust Issues 38
High Effort Starting Out 39
Maintenance Decisions 40
Dependence on Your Team 41
Tax Preparation 42

Chapter 4: Self Check-in 45
The First Step–Be Frank With Yourself and Decide What You Want ... 46
Risk vs. Reward 48
Protecting Yourself From….You! 51
    Procrastination 51
    Analysis Paralysis 52
    Control and Fear 52

Chapter 5: The Part Time REI Mindset 57
Expectations 58
Mistakes = Learning 60
Never Irreversible 61
Positivity Breeds Success 62

Chapter 6: Getting the Other Half on Board 65
Communication and Shared Discovery 66
Shared Goals and Purpose 67
Involving Your Partner in the Costs 67
Balancing It All Out 68
Some Myths About Investing To Share 69

Myth: Investing Will Lead To Loss of Security 69
Myth: Investing is Too Hard to Learn 69
Myth: It's Better To Stay In The Stock Market 69
Myth: It Takes Too Much Money and Time To Invest 70
Myth: Tenants and Clogged Toilets At 1 am 70

Chapter 7: The Tools and Processes Of the Successful Part-Time RE Investor 73
   Setting the Stage 74
   Systems and Processes 76
      Time Blocking 76
      Reminders, Alerts, and Checklists 77
      Fear-setting 77
      The One Thing 78
      Carefully Selected Goals and Deadlines 78
      Using Your Zero-Time 81
      Posting and Visual Reminders 82
      Get A Mentor 83
      Accountability and Punishments 84
      Leveraging Yourself 85
      Using Electronic Tools To Get What You Need Faster 85

Chapter 8: "Fun"damentals of RE Investing 89
   Markets and Cycles 90
   Returns and Indicators—Measures Of Success 99
   Your Private Residence vs. Rental Properties 101
      Financing 102
      To LLC or not to LLC 102
      1031 Exchanges 103
      Asset vs. Liability 103
      Creative Operation 104
      Expense Write-offs 104
      Rental Grade 105
      Location & Objective 105

Chapter 9: Taking Stock of Seeds 107
Financial Readiness 108
You May Have More Than You Think 108
Resource Readiness 110

Chapter 10: My Blueprint for Single-Family Success 113
Why Single Family? 114
Start With Your Criteria 115
Market Selection 117
    Jobs and Economic Outlook 118
    Market Cycles 119
    Government and Tenant Laws 119
    Personal Connections 120
    Amenities and Seasonality 120
Underwriting Rental Property 121
    Cash-Flow Underwriting 121
    Value Underwriting 124
To Turnkey or Not To Turnkey… 126
Decision Point on Turnkeys 129
Portfolio Building With Single Family Homes 133
    Standard Stacking 133
    HELOC Stacking 133
    Power Househacking 133
Buy, Rent, Rehab, Refinance, Repeat (BRRRR) 135
Overarching Single Family Philosophy 137

Chapter 11: Leveraging Others for Passive Multifamily Success 141
Why Multifamily? 141
    Recession-resistant 142
    We Are A Renter Nation 143
    Economies of Scale 145
    Financing and Control 146
    Cost Segregation 146
How Apartment / Commercial Buildings are Valued 147
Types and Ownership 149

Multifamily Syndications 150
    Returns and Measures of Success.. 154
    Cash-on-Cash 156
    Internal Rate of Return... 156
Selecting a Good Syndication Acquisition & Management Team ... 159
    How Did You Find Them?... 160
    How Do They Communicate? 160
    What Is Their Track Record?... 161
    Marketing Material?... 161
    Vertical Integration?... 161

Chapter 12: Your Turn… The Next Steps................................163
  Decision Time.. 164
  What Does Success Look Like For You? 166

About The Author 169

INTRODUCTION

DARE TO QUESTION YOUR REALITY

"The trouble with the rat race is that even if you win, you're still a rat." —Lily Tomlin

THE BIG QUESTION is: why did you pick up this book? Perhaps subconsciously you're drawn to this idea and never really thought investing part-time in real estate would be a realistic option for a busy person like yourself. Don't overthink it, because the answer will lead you to an infinitely better reality, fully determined by your own free will.

Throughout Steve Jobs' career at Apple, he acted on a philosophy of radical service to his customers where he provided them with something they didn't even know they needed. He exemplified his belief that businesses should be so in tune with their customers they can show them what they want before they realize it themselves.

This is my job. I want to show you that even as a full-time corporate or self-employed working professional, you deserve a life of financial independence, and you can get there through using the tried and true method of stable cash-flow real estate.

You may feel discomfort, apathy and acceptance, or maybe hopelessness and desperation in your financial situation and ultimate dependence on your job. Do you feel more like a hamster on a wheel than a self-standing individual? How about a cog in a machine within a corporate office where no one cares about your ideas and only points out your mistakes? How does it feel to not be able to take vacations any time you want to and be locked up in an office all day as the sun shines outside?

Vacations help us become more productive, giving some space to think, allowing the mind to expand creatively. We are adults, and yet we have lost control of when we can rest and when we can put the foot on the accelerator. In a corporate or high powered small business setting, sometimes we don't have the control to make that choice.

Whether you know it or not, invisible handcuffs are wrapped so tightly you can barely move. The "benefits" and "perks" of having a high-paying job or self-employment situation convinces you that the juice is worth the squeeze. Don't get me wrong here. While some of these are great for us in the short term, they are actually crutches that keep us dependent and, over time, feeling trapped. Much like eating fattening or overly sweet or salty food tastes amazing, the effects will put you in a comatose state which saps productive energy for the rest of the day. We should strive to rid ourselves of the temptations and complacency of the corporate shelter we are hiding under. The temptation to keep these golden handcuffs is very real.

We should not be craving this dependency on a corporate machine that views people as numbers. I know this struggle well.

When I used to get home from my job, I would simply plop down on the couch and turn off my brain. I was doing well at my job, but it wasn't rewarding. Looking back, if I was really busy at work and had a stressful day, it started out mostly because I didn't enjoy what I did at work. I remember doing many things in which the work could have been fun to do, but somehow got lost when I was asked to regurgitate repetitive information. Sometimes things were given to me that seemed tedious or monotonous and made the whole experience boring. I could feel my life force draining away due to boredom and it got even harder to concentrate in and out of the office.

I remember a time in which I was working as an engineer for an engineering contracting company. At the time, I had also started to get into personal development. Approaching my boss, I asked him to provide me with a bigger challenge.

"Hey John, do you have a minute to talk?" I poked around the corner of my boss' office pensively. "Sure, come on in." he gestured warmly. As I sat down, I felt a rush of confidence and excitement.

"I've been thinking about this for a long time. Are there any assignments that could take me into the field? I'm willing to travel as far as I need to. I'd like to work directly with clients."

My boss looked at me curiously, understanding that field position is hard work and often takes you far away from home for an extended time. I didn't care. I was 100% confident in myself and knew I could handle anything that was thrown at me. I foolishly went under the false pretense that if I poured my blood, sweat and tears into my work for over a year, adding immense value to both the company and the client, I would be rewarded.

Sadly, that never came to pass. I spent 8 hours in the field and another 3 or 4 in the client's office each day, doing all of the difficult, tedious work they didn't want to do themselves on-site for years. I expected a title promotion or a rate increase. In truth, I found out that I made less than my colleagues in the office, even while on assignment. I realized a few things in working for a company rather than working for yourself. It was there that I immediately decided I would not allow someone else to either directly determine my worth, misunderstand or take advantage of the value I'm adding. I can remember this frustration as clearly as if it were yesterday.

Don't get me wrong. I am thankful for all of the benefits and lessons my full-time jobs provided me. It's going forward with the understanding that there is a time and place for full time jobs. *Working full time for someone else should be a phase in life and not all of life.* Over the years, I've learned how to act on that mantra.

This book is for those dependent on jobs or trading their time and expertise as self-employed professionals for their financial well-being and want a change. We must rhetorically ask ourselves: how did it get this way? As someone alive in the most prosperous of eras in the modern world, why haven't we figured out this freedom of choice? I'd rather work very hard for 5–10 years and start to enjoy the fruits of my labor and my investments by getting my side hustle on! If this sounds familiar to you, you're in the right place.

Although you have a full-time job, it's possible to become financially independent from your employer or, if you are self-employed, escape the dreaded "time equals money" equation that Robert Kiyosaki refers to in his book, "Rich Dad Poor Dad." If you're able to find a way to help others by providing a clean and safe place to live, this is a valuable product that's almost always in demand. Real estate investing is truly possible for the average person, even if you're on a budget. I know this for a fact because I did it myself.

This side hustle can become your main gig over time. While it takes some energy and effort to start up, it is very rewarding and worthwhile. It's like a rocket ship that takes so much fuel to leave the atmosphere but becomes effortless once in space. I'm excited to be able to teach these principles and doing something this bold blesses the investor with the superpower attitude of self-determination and courage while adding value to others.

Life is supposed to be fun and interesting. It can also be challenging and rewarding. Escaping the corporate and self-employed hamster wheel enables you to make more choices and leads you to the way of complete financial independence. It will allow you to continue working, explore starting your own business, go back to school to learn more skills, or simply take a nice, long break. These choices are there for those willing to work up front for it, and this book will show you how to get there.

I remember one day staring at the student loan bill that I tore open in dismay when I landed my first real job in Houston. When I looked at it, I thought to myself, "What the heck is this?" as I sunk slowly into my living room chair. I knew I'd have to pay back student loans, but in college, I never even thought to do the math. After tossing the bill aside in disgust, I thought to myself, "How much in interest would I actually be paying on this stupid thing?" What I found was stunning: Two times my loan amount in interest. How could they do this?

I realized that for most students, the college student loan setup was a scam and lures students into signing up for debt when they have no idea how much they're actually paying. I found I was paying more than two times the loan's actual balance in interest payments if I decided to keep it. That was enough. I decided then and there I would pay it off as quickly as possible. Unfortunately, I had already bought a new car, moved into a swanky new apartment downtown and up to that point, had been eating out almost every night.

Gradually, I changed my habits, spending as little as possible while I tackled the debt. Looking back on the difficult 2½ years it took to pay off nearly $70,000 in student loan debt taught me a lot about how to manage money and control cash flow. These would be the foundational skills I would need to position myself for starting to invest in real estate.

Understanding interest rates, recurring expenses and the power of compound interest helped me build a strong portfolio of rental properties and multifamily properties over the years, all while working a full-time job and being happily married.

Ever since I was a little boy, I had a fascination with LEGOS and what I could build with them. I remember asking over and over again for more LEGOS so I could create anything, including a life-sized sword I may or may not have wanted to "try out" on some of my younger brother's toys. Over the years, I've realized this passion for creating and building things has stuck with me. In buy and hold real estate, each unit or house you acquire can be thought of as a single LEGO block. Eventually, if you can accumulate enough LEGO blocks, not only can you build a wall, but a plane, rocket ship, a car, or anything else in your imagination.

There is no one stopping you from building your fortress of LEGOS, except yourself. A full-time job or high-paying income as a self-employed individual will give you the foundation to go out and get more LEGO blocks, until your own LEGO blocks start to attract other blocks all on their own.

While you may think this takes a long time, I know from experience it doesn't have to. I started with a small amount of funds and turned that into a million-dollar portfolio in an out-of-state market in a very short period of time. These properties are leveraged and paying for themselves right now, but over some time, these investments will be the basis for an even larger portfolio. I've learned that real estate investing is not meant to make you rich immediately but a systematic approach will help you preserve and reliably grow your capital.

While we now have an idea of what will drive us and our general "why," let's take a closer look at how someone like me, a busy professional with no experience and tendency for over-analysis, was able to build a powerful investment portfolio part-time.

CHAPTER 1

LEGO BLOCKS AND MY STORY

"Don't wait to buy real estate. Buy real estate and wait." —Robert Allen

NOW THAT WE see there is a problem with the current status quo, I am determined to demonstrate to you how I'm freeing myself of long days in the office for a life of choice and self-determination. It is possible to do this in a relatively short time to create a cash flow portfolio that runs on its own.

From a 1,000 foot perspective, the goal is to have your portfolio run with minimal involvement on a day-to-day basis. If done correctly, it should take only 15-20 minutes per month. Before we learn more about stacking LEGO blocks to make this work, I'll share my story about how I got here, starting around five years ago in the mid 2010's.

PREPARATION & SELF GRATIFICATION

My wife and I started our investing career like many investors before us. Completely by accident.

She had purchased a condo in the Pacific Northwest one month before the huge real estate crash in 2008. When she finished medical school and looked to move to California to start her residency, the condo was still underwater and we couldn't sell in 2013. Out of options, we were forced to rent it to graduate students. These renters spoiled us because we didn't even need a property manager with them. We treated them well and they treated us nicely in return. We got used to the income coming in, which covered the mortgage and more. During our move to California, it got my gears turning. "Huh…" I thought to myself. "Why don't we get more of these?"

When I started off, my first goal was to get educated. I wanted to replicate this with the intention of rental property from the start. I listened to podcasts from Bigger Pockets and picked up countless books on the subject. Eventually the dreaded "analysis paralysis" settled in. It turned out real estate investing is insanely broad.

What resonated with me, and my "landlord-by-default" situation the most, was the LEGO block method of real estate investing, otherwise known as buy and hold. Just like purchasing dividend returning stock, buy and hold real estate is exactly as it sounds. You buy real estate, benefit from holding, and sell at an increased value later on. I loved the idea of accumulating LEGO blocks to build a foundation for my life of choice. Other forms of investing, such as flips and wholesaling, seemed like another full-time job to me.

We realized we were spending too much time analyzing and trying to find the perfect "deal" in my local market. It took some time, but we understood what really mattered: taking action. Shifting our focus from trying to hit a home run on our first purchase to learning and gaining skills and experience was the key. This took the pressure off us and we were able to purchase a property swiftly and logically.

TAKING THE PLUNGE

Some laminate flooring, trim, paint, and yard work transformed an abandoned property, owned by a bank, into an actual rental property in our local California market. Now, the hard and difficult lessons took hold. We learned how tenants damage your home, try to avoid being served court documents and even lie in court during eviction proceedings while producing forged evidence. We also learned we should have hired a property manager, but didn't because the numbers on the property were too thin to afford one. In the end, after we got the tenants out and sold the property in two years, we "flipped" it to ourselves by cleaning it out, and selling it, resulting in a net gain of around $120,000.

This, along with our nest egg of $40k from savings, became the basis for a number of single-family homes and small apartments and duplexes. If you're starting to panic about these numbers, don't. Even $10k–20k is enough to get started. You may even have more than you think, which we will discuss later. We literally started with nothing and built our team and portfolio from scratch. What helped was being plugged into a network of other real estate investors and getting a turnkey property or two from the get-go in a few of my target markets when starting out. This gave us the confidence to tell property managers and other investors that we already owned property and were looking to expand.

HEY, MAYBE THIS ISN'T SO BAD...

Some further research on Bigger Pockets, phone calls, and calendar invites later, I found myself meeting with 15-20 people on a business trip to my out-of-state markets. I understood it was the people who would connect me with the properties and rentals I needed to build my LEGO empire. The contacts I made helped me determine which sub-markets were good to look at and gave me a reference point for various downtown spots and local amenities. It was the catalyst for me finding my first package deal with a wholesale agent, who I had contacted through Bigger Pockets, then met in person.

After doing research and sharing what I was looking for with the wholesaler, a few weeks later he emailed me a package of five properties that perfectly fit my budget, all on the same street with a price tag of $200k. After getting some temporary funding in place, these rentals, already occupied, became ours. After a few repairs as well as light rehabs six months from purchase, my bank refinanced us into individual smaller loans with lower interest. Because the terms were so attractive, I still have these loans in place at the time of this writing. These loans are being paid off by the rents collected from tenants in these houses.

EXPANSION & BIGGER PLANS

We then looked to expand and sold our California property after going through a tiresome eviction, and converted it into cash-flow real estate via a 1031 exchange. This allowed me to move my $120k in California equity into a down payment for four more properties in my selected market.

Having gone through a stressful time to get properties identified, closed and stabilized, I was out of the cash I had saved and reached 10 mortgages in my name by the end of 2017. This took place in a timespan of about one year after starting my journey. My strategy was to obtain as much healthy debt (which involves other peoples' money and is able to be used for assets that fetch income) from rental properties as quickly as possible. This would allow me to have equity build while I determined my next move. I had also done research on multifamily properties and wanted to become an expert in this space for many reasons that we will get into later.

A year later, in 2018, a trip to the Midwest led us to a multifamily property, sourced from the original wholesalers who helped get our first properties in Indianapolis. This project launched me into the multifamily space, and I became enamored with the growth and scalability of multifamily properties.

When we closed our first multifamily commercial property, I was both elated and fearful. "Do you think we should do this?" I meekly asked my wife by phone, trying to convince ourselves this was a good move. "I believe in you. It will be great and you're probably going to regret it later if you don't. You got this!" This was exactly the confidence I needed to close on the 18-unit mixed use multi-plex.

I am grateful for all of the events that have led me to this day. While it seems like I planned this, that's hardly the case. Opportunities were there, I worked to seize them and simply followed the urge to create something to free me from my full-time job. It took focus and persistent action to get here, but has been well worth it.

I know that you can do it, too. I wouldn't be writing these words if I didn't have confidence that anyone can do it, including you.

WHAT'S IN OUR NEAR FUTURE TOGETHER

In the following pages, I want to share my insights as to how I was able to do all of this while working full time.

First, we're going to go over the advantages and disadvantages of investing in real estate with a full- time job. Next, we'll describe a successful part-time real estate investor and what kind of things can be expected when investing or starting the process.

It'll also be important to make sure your spouse or significant other and even your family understands and aligns with your vision. This is vitally important because, in addition to the basics on the property, you're actually learning to work with yourself, your loved ones and manage your own thoughts and expectations and attachments with money, risk, and investing.

After getting settled on the home front, we'll go over all the options you have to invest in real estate, and why I recommend buy and hold, in particular, for corporate and self-employed professionals. There will be links to various resources during this process to get more information and get you plugged into what you need or get answers to questions you may have. Finally, we will create an action plan, based on your goals and inspired by what you've learned.

I am excited to be with you on this journey and know you are fully capable of winning this game. While it may seem a little overwhelming right now, trust me when I say that it's worth the effort.

ACTION STEPS

➤ Jot down a few notes for why you're here. What made you get this book and why have you read to this point?

_____
_____
_____
_____
_____

➤ Picture yourself one year from now and you've done nothing different in your life. Where will you be? How does this make you feel?

_____
_____
_____
_____
_____

➤ Now imagine that you can wave a magic wand to make your goals come true, what would that look like and how does that make you feel?

_____
_____
_____
_____
_____

CHAPTER 2

ADVANTAGES OF REAL ESTATE AS AN INVESTMENT

"90% of all millionaires become so through owning real estate." —Andrew Carnegie

IT'S TIME FOR us to talk about what makes real estate as an investment so great. After all, why spend all this effort getting to know more about it without knowing it's decisive advantages? This chapter's material really lights me up. And if I've done my job correctly, it should do the same for you.

Real estate investing is such an underutilized yet powerful strategy to fuel your financial independence. Pretty soon, that will be abundantly clear. When I first learned about these advantages, I couldn't help but ask myself: "Why doesn't everyone do this?" Let's jump into it.

WHAT'S SO GREAT ABOUT REAL ESTATE?

Over the last millennium more millionaires and wealth has been created by real estate than any other asset class, according to the Federal Reserve Bank of San Francisco's Paper entitled "The Rate of Return on Everything, 1870–2015."[1] real estate demand remains high and tends to appreciate due to supply and demand. A rudimentary approach that made sense to me was this: as long as the population keeps increasing, people have to live somewhere. The number of units being built per year almost never matches the number of households needed, the scarcity creates upward velocity in prices and allows homes to retain their value, given the history of demand and supply. Figure 1 demonstrates this effect nicely.[2] According to Freddie Mac, the US economy is short by about 2.5 million housing units to match long-term demand, as of the end of 2018. The fastest pace of building in any year in the last two decades have been slower than the slowest years between 1968 and 2007.[3]

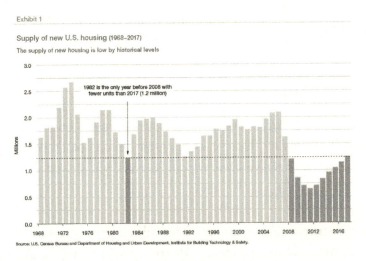

Figure 1

---

1   https://www.frbsf.org/economic-research/files/wp2017-25.pdf.
2   https://www.kansascityfed.org/en/publications/research/eb/articles/2019/escaping-housing-shortage
3   http://www.freddiemac.com/research/insight/20181205_major_challenge_to_u.s._housing_supply.page?

Most professionals have significant assets in paper holdings, with a fairly large amount of that held in instruments traded in Wall Street (Figure 2). According to the Federal Reserve Survey of Consumer Finances from 2016, most professionals with a net worth between $100,000 and $1,000,000 hold anywhere between 30% and 40% of their net worth in stocks, bonds and retirement accounts.[4]

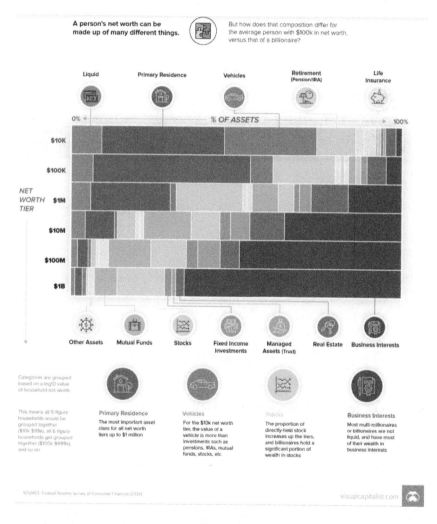

Figure 2

---

4   https://www.visualcapitalist.com/chart-assets-make-wealth/

While this does have a place in your portfolio and investment strategy, diversifying with real estate can help you decrease your risk and build a stronger financial foundation. According to the real estate research company Nuveen, private real estate diversification increases returns on a risk-adjusted basis better than investing in (Real Estate Income Trusts) REITs which operate much like a mutual fund, only the focus is on larger commercial property. See Figure 3 for more details.[5]

Private real estate offered better risk-adjusted returns than listed REITs.

Combining both categories improved performance

1998-2018	PRIVATE REAL ESTATE	LISTED REITs	COMBINED (80% private real estate/ 20% listed REITs)
Total returns (average annual)	8.6%	8.5%	9.0%
Volatility (standard deviation)	11.2%	19.5%	10.1%
Risk-adjusted returns (Sharpe ratio)	0.51	0.35	0.59

Data for the period 01 Jan 1998 – 31 Dec 2018. The indexes represented are as follows: U.S. private real estate (NCREIF Fund Index – Open End Diversified Core Equity (NFI – ODCE), listed REITs (FTSE Nareit U.S. Real Estate Index). Performance over different time periods may have been less favorable than shown above. It is not possible to invest in an index. Performance for indices does not reflect investment fees or transaction costs.

Source: MacroBond

Figure 3

Fortunately, real estate has got your back here, too.

---

5   https://www.nuveen.com/en-us/thinking/real estate/global-real-estate-opportunity-for-income-and-diversification

OUTLOOK

The outlook for residential real estate is amazing. Projections vary, based on the type of real estate such as single-family homes or apartments, offices, industrial, retail, or raw land on the commercial side. There are two primary demographic groups contributing to the high demand in rental units:

- *Millennials* seeking urban and mobile lifestyles while drowning in student loan debt desire access to amenities and
- *Baby Boomers* who are selling their homes and moving into rental units to live a better lifestyle with on-demand medical services, along with a higher sense of community, quality of life and nicer weather.

Migration between states with better tax advantages, cost of living differences and weather perks are also drawing people to certain areas of the country.

At the time of this writing, COVID-19 is ravaging the financial system. Unemployment has reached levels not seen since the Great Depression and the Federal Reserve is printing more than $2 trillion into the economy to keep the system from unraveling.[6] What this will do to housing is difficult to predict in the near to medium term, but we do expect to see strong inflationary forces eventually make its way to the world stage. When that happens, those holding assets like cash flowing real estate will reap huge benefits. Because of the mortgage system behind much of the housing in the US, the near future of real estate is a mixed bag. On the other hand, the need for physical space is common among all human beings, therefore, real estate has a great long term outlook. Obtaining property in times like this in the past (as in the 2008–2009 meltdown) have yielded huge opportunities for investors like you and me.

---

6   https://www.nytimes.com/2020/04/09/business/economy/fed-economic-rescue-coronavirus.html

RELIABLE DEMAND

Real estate as an asset class is a reliable source of income. Everyone needs a place to live. Shelter is one of the most basic human needs in society, outside of food and water, and being in this business means you will be providing this service.

OPTIONS

The options when investing in real estate are dizzying. There's the ability to invest capital with improvements in properties, then deploy your equity, refinance, sell or partner with anyone. The assets can, like any other paper-based commodity, be placed in entities and purchased with little to nothing down. Sometimes, if you can find a property good enough, you can even net cash back to you at closing.

ACQUISITION

Additional advantages for real estate include being able to use your Individual Retirement Account (IRA) or retirement funds to invest in properties. This is a huge benefit, because, if you were like me, you didn't even know you could use your hard-earned retirement funds to invest in real estate until you sought advice. In some cases, even funds you bring into your 401(k) or 403(b) may be eligible for rolling into an IRA or Qualified Retirement Plan (QRP) to invest in property. Information on these types of accounts can be found in the Book Resources section of our website found in Chapter 9. You lose a few advantages buying property this way (such as being able to write off expenses or being able to leverage your money with loans), but the benefits outpace the disadvantages. See Figure 4 for a look at some top pro's and con's for buying property inside your IRA.

As a side note, I personally dipped my own toes into investing out of state with my IRA. I had a large balance I had saved up in my personal IRA. My first property was purchased with retirement funds from previous employers. I bought it all cash in my new target market of Indianapolis back in late 2016. Flying out to the market, I was taken by a turnkey operator on a bus tour with many other cash investors looking for a return. The tour was a big show, and that's about it. It was, however, impressive enough for me to decide to purchase a property. It has become the poorest performing property in my entire portfolio to this day. Many other investors who were brought in also echoed this statement. It did, however, get me started in hands-on investing and gave me a point of reference as to what worked and what didn't. Regardless, if you follow the guidelines in this book, you can do very well in your IRA's by using real estate as a vehicle and can start quickly if you have sizable amounts saved in retirement funds.

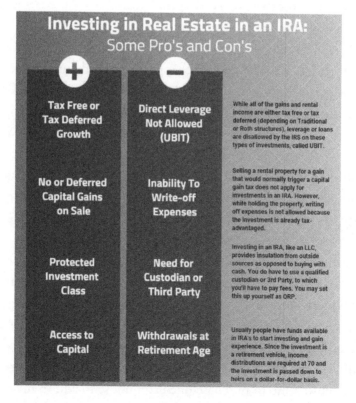

Figure 4

1031 EXCHANGES

There is also a mechanism called a 1031 Exchange in which, if you sell one rental property you can exchange it and defer the capital gains taxes you otherwise would have had to pay if you sold the property without using this exemption. This is huge because it can essentially help defer taxes so you will never pay it. You'll leave the property to your heirs on a stepped-up basis, and the deferred gains accumulated over the years vanish. There are limitations to using this technique, such as needing to disclose to the buyer/seller that you are doing a 1031 which puts you at a negotiating disadvantage (also due to the short timeframe in which you'll have to identify and close property). With the right planning, it's a great method to deploy and grow all 100% of your accumulated equity. We will cover more on this later to show how powerful using 1031's can be. Always be sure to consult a 1031 specialist for more advice and specific details on how this works.

My wife and I used a 1031 Exchange to expand our buy and hold portfolio out-of-state when we sold one property in our local market. The process is admittedly cumbersome with fees and extra paperwork under a tight deadline, especially for your first time doing it. When we sold our California rental house, we had a 1031 exchange company, referred to as a "custodian," hold the sale funds for us. While they held the funds, they allowed us a short 45 days after the house closed to *identify* property to purchase with the proceeds. Even though we had 120 days to *close* on them, it was a stressful time with lots of underwriting analysis, frantic calls to agents, wholesalers and contractors in order to meet the *identification* deadline. Eventually, we settled in on two houses from one agent and one house and a fourplex from another, just in time to meet the 45 day identification deadline. Looking back on how this chaotic process unfolded, buying properties this way with a 1031 exchange was stressful. It didn't have to be, though if I had planned for it better. In any event, it allowed me to purchase one extra house to add to my portfolio rather than pay Uncle Sam's capital gains taxes with it.

If you are curious to learn more about this method of deferring capital gains tax, more information can be found in the Resources section of our website.

TAX ADVANTAGES

Adding real estate into your portfolio can give you a decisive edge in tax planning. Most Americans who work W-2 jobs contribute on average 24% of their gross pay to different tax types such as income, property, sales and so on.[7] With a successful real estate portfolio, you are cash flow positive while actually reporting a paper loss to the IRS. When I first started investing in real estate, I didn't really notice this effect, but once my portfolio took off, we started to enjoy five-figure refund checks from the IRS. There are several books and resources written on this subject and I don't claim to be a tax professional or CPA, but have seen firsthand what real estate portfolios do for me in this area.

BUSINESS STATUS

Related to the tax benefits from real estate investing is the "business nature" given by the IRS, regardless of the entity. This will take form as either Schedule E, if held in your name, or K-1 if held in an LLC. As a business, you pay taxes on the bottom line only after all of your expenses, mortgage interest, and depreciation are considered. You have the ability to control these things to offset certain tax situations in your personal life by using your real estate. For example, if I were to cash out of my 401(k) as a withdrawal in the early part of the year, that would count as taxable income. I could then offset that by placing more debt on my properties, assuming I have the equity to do so. I'd then pay more in mortgage interest,

---

[7] https://www.usatoday.com/story/money/taxes/2018/04/25/how-much-does-the-average-american-pay-in-taxes/34138615/

which would help offset that early withdrawal and increase in tax burden. If this is hard to follow, don't worry, it'll come naturally to you later.

Whenever I travel to my market and meet with my property managers, I get to write off the entire trip as a business expense. If you happen to have family in that city, the IRS will give you the benefit of allowing you to travel to the area to do business and check up on your rental. Your trip will then be written off against your income. In addition, there are several times in which my wife and I talk about real estate or business over a meal / night out at the town, and having a portfolio of properties legitimizes that conversation, which allows us to write off the meal. Again, please consult with a tax professional on this, because I am definitely not one.

PASSIVE INCOME

Another advantage touches on the LEGO block nature of real estate investing. This means you can control your income streams better than if you had to rely on the stock market for your income. For example, if you know that you need $8,000 per month income for your family to live comfortably and to be able to continue to invest, you can break this up into a number of properties or "doors."

If you find you are able to generate about $200 per door per month on average, that will make your goal $8,000 / $200 = 40 units to reach your desired result. The rental income you receive each month normally has a fixed value as a return back to you, and will increasingly do so as you build your portfolio of units to help cover repairs, vacancies and so on. I find this appealing because it allows you to reach a tangible and easily pictured goal.

Once you are there, it is yours. If you tried this approach in the stock market, the numbers are not as much in your favor throughout the market cycles. When stocks are doing well, the numbers when selling look great and dividend returns are high. But as of the recent market impacts at the time of this writing, the stock market has taken an inevitable downturn due to the COVID-19 impacts on discretionary spending. This simply highlights the unpredictability and lack of control on returns that is characteristic of the stock market. If you are heavily invested in dividend yielding stocks and mutual funds, your dividend payments also start to decrease and you will have to start selling your nest egg to make up for the missing income you depend on to live.

With real estate, you have more options. If rental income starts slowing, you can sell off properties in a cool market if needed. A refinance or some other creative transaction could also help ease your situation. Typically there are more options available than if you held all your financial positions in paper assets such as stocks and bonds.

HEDGE ON INFLATION

Real estate is a perfect hedge against inflation. See Figure 5 for a visual on inflation versus real estate Net Operating Income.

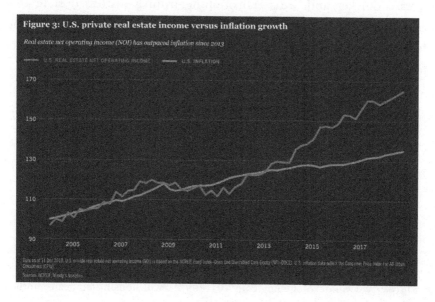

Figure 5

As more money is pumped into the economy, the proportion of wealth of households, relative to their net worth grows rapidly in their primary residence. A look at Figure 6 below reveals that the average American in the US holds a large amount of their net worth at retirement age in their home equity, and that the increase of values in the home equity translates to an increase in their net worth, according to Census Data.[8]

Age Range	Net Worth	Net Worth (Excluding Equity in Own Home)	Total Assets at Financial Institutions	Total Equity in Own Home
Households Aged 45-54	$104,300	$38,590	$4,085	$75,000
Households Aged 55-64	$178,300	$70,880	$6,000	$120,000
Households Aged 65 and older	$201,500	$59,780	$8,025	$140,000
Households Aged 65-69	$197,500	$69,600	$6,700	$130,000
Households Aged 70-74	$218,200	$73,040	$7,500	$139,000
Households Aged 75 and Older	$193,600	$49,370	$10,000	$145,000

Figure 6

As more money is printed, home values increase. Areas more desirable increase quicker and areas transitioning from a distressed state to a desirable one, due to market job growth and demand, rise in value. Home prices also tend to increase in a more stable manner than the stock market as shown in Figure 7.[9]

---

8   https://goodlifehomeloans.com/average-american-net-worth-at-retirement/
9   https://www.indexologyblog.com/2015/09/01/will-housing-be-dealt-another-bad-hand/

Exhibit 2: The S&P 500 and the S&P/Case-Shiller U.S. National Home Price Index

Source: S&P Dow Jones Indices LLC and CoreLogic. Past performance is no guarantee of future results. Chart is provided for illustrative purposes and reflects hypothetical historical performance.

Figure 7

Additionally, the debt payments behind them can be fixed at rates advantageous to the owner who is able to capitalize on them. At the time of this writing, the Unied States government has pumped over $2 trillion into the economy in a matter of weeks, which will eventually lead to inflationary forces in the future along with the additional stimulus monies that are sure to come. The growth of goods and services offered in the open market will more or less keep the same trajectory with a much larger amount of dollars in the market, leading to the dilution of the dollars that are already out there. If you have fixed debt from real estate or another asset class, the value of the asset will keep up with inflation, but the debt you pay behind it will remain fixed at older dollars, pegged against lower prices when you originally purchased the asset.

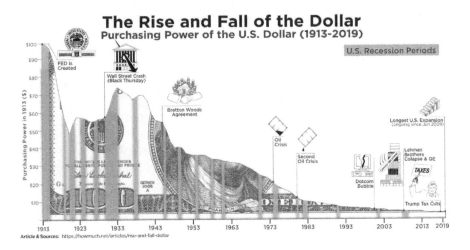

Figure 8

Figure 8 depicts just how strong that effect can be over time. The spending power of the US dollar has dramatically changed over the last 100 years.[10]

OUTPERFORM ANY OTHER ASSET CLASS

Real estate simply outperforms stocks. There are few other investment options in the world where infinite cash-on-cash rates of return are possible. This may seem pretty far fetched, but I have done it myself and will show you exactly how to do this. While the uninitiated in real estate investing would incorrectly assume that a REIT or the Schiller case home index is a great way to compare true real estate performance versus the S&P 500 or the Dow Jones, it does not.

Often, stock professionals and financial planners can only see homes and apartment buildings as stock themselves by looking purely only at the property itself. They naively assess their value, compared to what

---

10   https://howmuch.net/articles/rise-and-fall-dollar

the market prices them. Appreciation of property, by holding it over a period of time is only one way in which real estate delivers value. What about rental income, leverage, and other income forms? Since these are all personal and hard to measure, it's impossible to compare to the stock market so this comparison is often meaningless unless these are also being considered in the analysis.

Here are five ways in which you make money in real estate. Refer to Figures 9 through 13 for an example of what each of these benefits look like separately.

APPRECIATION

This is the simple gain in home value over time due to supply and demand. In single-family and small multifamily apartment buildings, the value of the property is determined by the surrounding properties. Let's assume you purchased a property a year ago. If a house on your street sells for around $10k higher than what you bought it for and it is similar in size, square feet and finishes, the odds are good your property has also increased in value. For example, if you purchased a home for $100k and your market has been averaging price increases of about 3-5% per year, you can expect your home to be worth anywhere from $110k–$120k in three years.

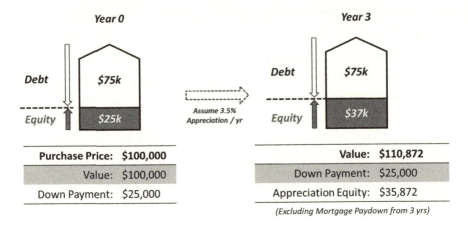

Figure 9

EQUITY CAPTURE

Although "equity capture" sounds fancy, it is simply another term for "buying at a discount." Because real estate investing is dependent on many factors and has a businesslike nature, you can help serve a need by closing for a seller who needs to sell quickly. Reasons vary, be it divorce, death in the family, or something else. If you encounter this situation and offer assistance to solve it, that same $100k house explained in the example above may be able to be purchased for $80k–$85k. If it all works out, you have created around $15-$20k in equity for yourself by getting a $100k property for only $85–$80k. Try doing that with stocks and bonds!

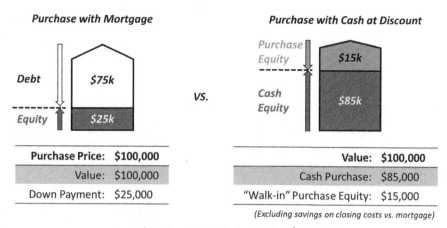

Figure 10

DEPRECIATION

This one is huge. The IRS wants you to own real estate because they want people who have the ability to manage property and improve it for the good of the country. They want this so much, they'll let you depreciate your property, claiming it is being "used up," much like an office copier machine, computer, etc. in your business. It can be referred to as "phantom" cash flow because it is real but not seen. As you hold your property, the IRS essentially gives you a break on using up your assets in your business as well as your property, and gives an allowance for the time you've held it as an expense.

Remember: you pay taxes on your income minus your expenses, so the more expenses you identify, the further you will offset your income. This calculation is based on the amount you paid to acquire it from the beginning. With single-family homes, most investors use straight-line calculations which provide the same depreciation expense each year for 27.5 years. In multifamily, you are able to do cost segregation analysis, which allows you to fully depreciate your building in a shorter period of time, usually between five and twelve years, which leads to massive tax savings early on.

If you're confused about how this works, let's quickly look at an analogy. Consider how your car depreciates in value over the years you've owned it along with the number of miles driven. This loss of value each year is the car's depreciation because you are "using it up." When the car is completely used up, it's value is either zero or close to it, and the entire asset should be replaced and has no value to the open market. In the case of property, the government allows you to estimate the same "cost of using the property up" each year, assuming that the property will be all used up, having no more useful life to give. We know this isn't true since property usually has much larger life cycles than cars do and eventually rise in value (Appreciation). This is one of the ways that Uncle Sam tells us that he wants us to invest in real estate.

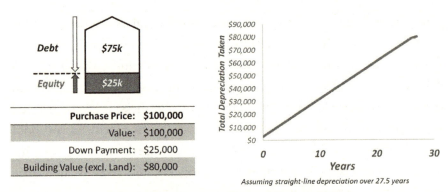

Figure 11

CASH FLOW

This is simply the rental income you receive from your properties. If you are able to generate a positive cash flow each month from your rental portfolio after paying your debt service, you are cash-flow positive and can benefit from more rentals. Most buy-and-hold investors look to prioritize this value component when looking for property.

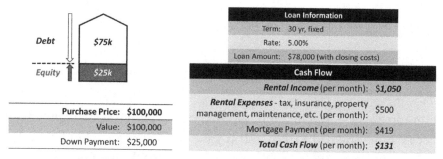

Figure 12

DEBT PAYDOWN

One of the most appealing aspects of holding property is that debt remains fixed while income and property value usually increase over time. Your tenants pay all your expenses and your debt. This debt paydown, that compounds over time, increases your bottom line. Your tenants are paying down your debt which adds to your overall net worth by reducing what you owe to your lender.

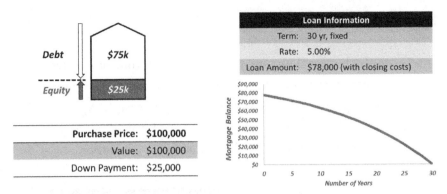

Debt Paydown Gains: $1,174 first yr (up to $4,832 in final mortgage year)

Figure 13

How do all these benefits work together on a typical real estate purchase? Let's assume you had $100k cash at your disposal as shown in Figure 14. This could allow either $100k in stocks, one $100k cash house purchase or 4–5 x $100,000 houses with leverage and down payments.

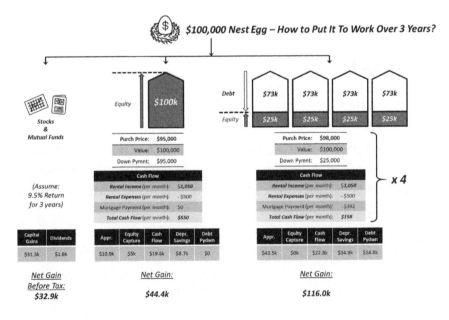

Figure 14

If you take the leveraged option and happen to find a tremendous deal due to your hard-working agent, let's say lock up four houses at a value of $85k each, which need $5k of work and $5k in closing costs. If the houses retail at $100k each, you have received *Equity Capture* of ($100k–($85k + $5k + $5k)) x 4 houses = $20k. Because you were able to rent these houses at a fair rate, your tenants are paying your mortgage for you (*Debt Paydown*) and you are getting a small profit each month after reserves for vacancies and CAPEX (*Cash Flow*). Over time, you claim *Depreciation* and pay less taxes on your Federal Tax return than your colleagues at your 9-5 job due to the "phantom losses" you've claimed, even though you have net cash in your pocket. And after the first year, because you've magnified the number of assets you control by using leverage, you benefit from appreciation by four times instead of one if you had just purchased one house outright with cash. Each of the houses go up in value by 4% in year one, and at the end of the year, you've created $4k in *Appreciation* on each house, even though there is debt on the properties and you put down only $25k for each property. Appreciation alone is providing you a 16% return in your first year for each house ($4k gained / $25k out-of-pocket spend).

This is really amazing stuff, and, once I understood these benefits, I was a true believer.

PROVIDING A HOME FOR A FAMILY THAT NEEDS IT

When you start building a business, you are in the business of providing people a safe and comfortable place to live. Take pride in the fact that you are contributing to the social, cultural and physical well-being of the people in your property. By running your portfolio in an ethical way by maintaining your property and caring for your tenants, you stand apart from other landlords and make a difference to people who need it and the community. This business allows you to directly impact peoples' lives for the better. The best landlords are ones in a harmonious business relationship with their tenants and property managers.

INTANGIBLE BENEFITS OF INVESTING IN REAL ESTATE

When adding another LEGO block to my empire, I feel extremely accomplished, knowing I've moved that much closer to financial independence. This gives me a huge confidence boost and the sense that I'm able to take life into my own hands.

I used to possess a perfectionist streak that is much quieter now thanks to real estate investing. I now understand things go wrong and can accept it. Problems that once worried me, I shrug off, work through them and, if needed, allow the space for creativity to resolve the issue. I embrace the mantra that "if it would be easy, everyone would be doing it."

As time goes on, you start to see things that seemed so far away, such as complete control of your time, becoming a reality. As you measure income coming in, you start fantasizing about what it would be like to have that income replace the paycheck from your employer with much less ongoing work and time involvement. Visualizing this motivation drives me to push on in the hardest times.

When you're in this game, you're not in it alone. By talking to other investors, you learn about exciting markets, techniques, approaches, philosophies, etc. You develop your B.S. detector since there's plenty of it out there. You will pay attention to what appeals to you and your investing style, and find people who do what you do. You'll be drawn towards them and potentially even work together to unlock worlds you never knew existed.

You'll meet some incredible people and get to travel and see some interesting places and properties. While travelling and discovering new places to invest, you come across people that you may relate to especially well. You'll get a chance to talk to people from all walks of life and broaden your horizons. This was the case with me when I took my second trip out to Indianapolis. There my wife and I met a young man and his wife at Starbucks downtown. He was just getting started in investing in property. Since then, we've kept in touch and he's built up a sizable portfolio himself. Over time, we started to build a long term relationship in helping each other. He is turning out to be a strong business partner.

These are just some intangibles you may or may not experience as you become a part-time real estate investor. Over time, this will turn you into a person capable of keeping focus on investing in the long run, which is how wealth and freedom is built. We see this in a microcosm of author, podcaster, coach, and ex-military leader Jocko Willink's observations that "discipline equals freedom." Just as working hard now will allow you to work not so hard later, the inverse is true as well.

And while this looks good now, real estate investing is still a business, with ups and downs. The highs are real, but the lows can be extremely painful when starting out. In the next chapter, we need to get real and understand there are challenges that may materialize that don't occur in other forms of passive investing. The advantages far outweigh the disadvantages but it's important to understand both sides of the equation. We owe it to ourselves to realize what we are getting ourselves into when things don't go so great so that we can fight through it and continue to build our wealth and grow as investors.

ACTION STEPS

➤ What are the five ways in which you can make money in real estate? Write them in the blanks below.

_____

_____

_____

_____

_____

➤ Consider where you live right now. Think about how much you could rent it for 5 years ago and what you could rent it for now. If you already rent, think about how much your place could have been purchased for 5 years ago. If you live in an apartment, find a nearby single-family home in Zillow for the sake of the exercise.

➤ For each way of making money in the blanks below, estimate the value of each income method you wrote down if you had purchased the house you're living in now 5 years ago (or the house you've selected on Zillow). Just approximate with mental math, no need to be specific. Later on, we'll provide examples on how to calculate it all.

1.) _____   Guess Value: $ _____
2.) _____   Guess Value: $ _____
3.) _____   Guess Value: $ _____
4.) _____   Guess Value: $ _____
5.) _____   Guess Value: $ _____

Next, add up the value of all the methods in which you can make money on rental real estate.

TOTAL VALUE: $ _____

➢ Considering that discipline equals freedom, what things can you work on inside yourself to help you take advantage of all the possibilities of real estate investing?

_____
_____
_____
_____
_____

CHAPTER 3

DISADVANTAGES OF REAL ESTATE INVESTMENTS

"Being challenged in life is inevitable, being defeated is optional." —Roger Crawford

WHILE THE PICTURE I've painted up to now is nothing but optimistic, there is a downside to real estate investments that potential investors must be aware of. In this chapter, we'll discuss risks that have materialized in some way or form in my experiences in real estate investing. If you decide to take the single-family route discussed in future chapters, this will especially apply to you.

When my wife and I set out to build our portfolio by purchasing a rental property in California, we bought a bank-owned property that sat vacant for a few years. The property needed a complete trashout, landscaping, new flooring, a coat of paint, ducting, and plumbing work. We worked many long weekends together on that property, doing most of the work ourselves. After work was done, we screened out and walked through prospective tenants who, when selected, said "thanks for taking a chance on us." That was the first red flag.

We then started to get rent checks… but only for a few months. After not paying rent while we still had to pay the mortgage, we asked them to leave if we gave them "cash for the keys." The next tenant was even worse, pretending that they were sick and in the hospital, avoiding being served eviction documents, presenting forged signatures in eviction court and accusing us of allowing the garage door to "crush" them. These were professional tenants who had done this before and slightly changed their names each time they applied for a place to live. This is why there was no credit or eviction history on them. We learned our lesson the hard way through this property. It was time for us to graduate our perspective from being a hobby to being a business.

The goal of this chapter is to make you understand that while real estate is the superior asset class, it's also the one that requires the right kind of person to understand the risks and navigate management of the asset. Simply put, it is work, especially when first starting out. Here are some ways in which it can test you and push the bounds of your resiliency.

RESPONSIBILITY

No matter what happens to the property, you are ultimately responsible for addressing the issues. If taxes aren't paid because you got too busy to put it on auto-pay, that's on you. If the city fines you because your tenant is not mowing the grass, that's also on you. In some cities, the utilities are actually kept in your name and the tenant is expected to pay each month. If the tenants don't pay, the city will still send you the bill. Your property manager is your biggest defender here, but if they don't do their job, it's still on you.

Going one step further, if your tenant decides not to pay rent one month because they instead spent it on Christmas gifts, your mortgage company won't care. You may have to foot the bill until you and/or your property manager fix the issue. There may be months in which you are cash-flow negative because of repairs or because your tenants got behind in rent. Fortunately for us, these problems are usually preventable and do not happen overnight, but rather emerge as something minor and then patterns emerge.

Ways to mitigate (see Resources Section for more information on all mitigation measures mentioned in this chapter):

- Conservative Underwriting (more on this later in future Chapters)
- Use LLC's or land trusts if possible
- Get a great property manager (PM)

ILLIQUIDITY / LOSS OF DIRECT CONTROL

When going through the process of identifying and purchasing your first rental investment, you may find there is lots of paperwork and this can be pretty tedious. This starts from the price and terms negotiation, to disclosures, inspections, loan underwriting and more. If things go south, you'll be on the other side of the table, selling and going through the same process, which usually lasts 30–45 days. Sometimes, this can be short-circuited if you are willing to sell at a steep discount, often to another investor or wholesaler.

One of the best ways to purchase property is to do so out of state if you live in an expensive housing market. A common objection I hear in doing this is that it rules out the ability of you driving to the property. Many investors starting out feel they need to be more hands-on with their investment. Although this is a real fear for many starting out, it's not advisable to think this way. It is your property manager and agents who can do this job for you. Be honest with yourself: will you know what you're looking at once you're there, or are you simply placating yourself? Will you really want to drive by the house any time there is an issue? Once again, this sounds like another job to me.

One last consideration is once you put your money down, most likely it will be "stuck" in the property for the short term, unless you are buying a property with significant Equity Capture that would allow you to take your cash out in the short term. While we recommend individuals wait until they are ready to invest, sometimes emergencies happen and your funds are not as easily available as if they were in the stock market.

Ways to mitigate:

- Plan to hold enough cash in reserve (Exactly how much? More on this later).
- Have a great property manager.

REHAB BUDGET OVERRUNS OR TRUST ISSUES

This happens almost all the time during heavy rehabs, a frustrating situation if you are just starting out. It's not easy to accept when the contractor you found takes your money and proceeds to send you pictures of a different property he is working on, reporting the "progress" on your property. Sometimes contractors will understate their budget and cut corners. Other times, unexpected issues come up when the walls are opened. It may require additional funds and it may take longer than expected. Meanwhile, you are feeding the debt service on the property if you're using leverage. This is part of the difficult stabilization phase on your property. I'll say it again: you will always come out ahead if you hold long enough. You will also be sure not to make the same mistake again on the next property.

Ways to mitigate:

- Get multiple contractor quotes.
- Be realistic and have cash for 50%–100 past your rehab budget on reserve.
- Have your PM or agent involved to drive by and take pictures and video during renovations.

HIGH EFFORT STARTING OUT

It takes time to get started in this business. After all, you are taking the time to read this book at the start of your journey. If you decide to do this yourself, and start in a single-family or multifamily yourself, the learning curve is much higher, but your education will turn you into a more savvy investor. Starting as a passive investor and joining other people's larger multifamily property investments will help you get there as well, but you'll be more dependent on those folks as time goes by. Only you know which route is for you.

Buying property is hard and in order to find the right investment, you have to analyze and sift through your options. Once you purchase, you'll spend the next month or two getting the property ready for rent and actually collecting rent from your tenants. After purchasing the property your work has just begun, because you'll oftentimes need to:

- Clean it out (if needed)
- Perform rehab or repairs that were identified in the inspection reports
- Pay and track your contractors doing the work
- Take final pictures and set pricing with your property manager
- List and begin marketing the property
- Screen prospects (done by your property manager)
- Host a showing (done by your property manager)
- Interview finalists (done by your property manager)

After all of this takes place with your guidance, teamed up with your property manager, you'll have your tenant. This alone can be a tough experience, especially with a full-time job. Once you have it rented, things get much simpler and you've earned your LEGO block. The next time, as you can imagine, will be much easier.

Along with working with the right people, you must constantly educate yourself because real estate is so intricately tied to local and national economies that constantly change and evolve. In recent years, there has been a technological transformation rapidly changing the space to be more competitive in property acquisition and operation. Being up-to-date is essential so you are aware of your tenants' needs, how your PM is doing and how well you are managing your portfolio. Learning will never stop because as a real estate investor, you are also a business man / woman. Occasionally you may have to fly out to your market to show face, meet local investors and grow your reach and influence to add value.

Ways to mitigate:

- Consistent practice.
- Network with other investors.
- Be honest and patient with yourself.

MAINTENANCE DECISIONS

This is what mostly comes to mind when people hesitate about buying rentals. There will be times where you'll just need to replace that furnace. I've had, for example, A/C units, stoves, drain lines, electrical, plumbing and roofs suddenly needing to be fixed. Be assured that as long as you are getting multiple quotes and opinions and trusting your PM's advice, addressing the issue will likely resolve it for many years. In order to cut down on expensive repairs like this, it is *highly* recommended you pay attention to the inspection report. When you first purchase the property, do yourself a favor and factor repairs and replacements into your overall purchase expense.

A few months after closing a five-property single-family house package, my property manager called. "I hate to deliver this news, but there's a major plumbing issue and sewage is coming up from the lawn and into the house." I was silent as I tried to process this, my anxiety growing. "It's a tree," my property manager told me. "The roots have wrapped around the sewer line and now we have to trench all the way to the sidewalk and replace the entire line." My heart sank as we worked through the details. About $5,000 later, the issue was resolved. In this case, I didn't have time to worry because my property manager found a solution and worked to resolve it. It was just a matter of money at this point. As it turned out, I had failed to address this item from the inspection report.

Yes, it was my fault, but it was a well-earned lesson and you can bet I'll never make this mistake again. Other issues also started to appear with other properties, but as time went on, I became more determined and knew that sticking with it would allow me to win in the long game.

Ways to mitigate:

- Address items in inspection reports from closing.
- Avoid temporary solutions: get to the root of the problem and address it.
- Ask for multiple quotes from your property manager.
- Purchase properties 50 years old or newer.

DEPENDENCE ON YOUR TEAM

Another "downside" that could introduce risks into your business is the need for others to operate for you. Your property manager and agents are essential, so you really have to make sure they will be working on your side. They need to be incentivized to stay with you and do their best work to serve you. With property managers, you have to monitor their fees for leasing, turnover, and management as well as assess if they are really worth their salary. On the multifamily side, you must trust the managers of the investment to run the team as you see fit and ensure communication is clear.

Over the duration of my career as an investor, I've realized the "downside" of having a team is not really a downside. You are actually employing people and trusting them, which allows you to do more of what you do best rather than trying to do everything yourself. As long as your team is worthy of your trust, you can expand your holdings toward rapid success.

Ways to mitigate:

- Interview and research performance of PM's, agents and multifamily general managers closely.
- Ask for sample agreements and fee lists.

TAX PREPARATION

I've only included this last point because your tax returns will become slightly more complicated. You may get to a point where hiring a tax professional (CPA) who focuses on real estate investments can help you to maximize the benefits of real estate investing. They can even offer advice and answer any questions on what would help make the most sense if you decide to buy, upgrade, sell, or exchange your investments. This expertise does involve more time, money, and energy on your end but having a great CPA will help you save money at tax time. The best CPA's, in many cases, also can pay for themselves (and more) versus doing taxes yourself, and give you perspective from their own experiences in working with other investors as well.

Despite these difficulties and risks, I must re-emphasize that *it is worth it*. The challenges are common to all investors and when you face them one day, know you will grow from the experience. Keep things in perspective and understand that real estate investing is akin to cooking with a crockpot compared to a microwave for building wealth. Learning and making mistakes is part of the process and should be expected.

In the next chapter, we'll do a check to see where you are and find out what kind of investor you should be.

ACTION STEPS

➢ Consider which of these difficulties is the most concerning to you. What would be the "worst case" scenario in your mind for that area?

_____
_____
_____
_____

➢ Think about what you may be able to do to prevent or mitigate this risk from happening. List any other additional ways to help you overcome this.

_____
_____
_____
_____

➢ Whatever else you are worried about, understand that other people starting out have had the same concerns. There are resources out there to help you with any challenge you may have. List these other concerns here. By the end of the book, you may learn something that addresses these for you. We'll refer back to this later on.

_____
_____
_____
_____

CHAPTER 4

SELF CHECK-IN

"You cannot always control what goes on outside, but you can always control what goes on inside." —Wayne Dyer

IN THIS CHAPTER, it's time to take inventory on yourself.

We have now seen the ways in which investing in real estate, while working full time, can be advantageous to your financial foundation as well as other ways where it can pose a challenge. When I first bought numerous properties, I was exhilarated by the prospect of owning multiple rental listings, but within a month, the furnaces broke down and needed to be replaced. With $4,000 in repairs and replacements, I wondered how I was going to pay for this and started freaking out. I worried that future properties would have further issues but that day never came.

You learn to grow and deal with these fluctuations as discussed in the last chapter.

It's time to get honest and decide if we are truly ready to go into the rental business. First, we'll start with various awareness tools to help understand where you are and give an honest assessment of your mental readiness as well as understand which approach to rental real estate might be best for you. Next, we need to ask questions about what is really important to you and form goals, even if they are small. After that, we'll take a small detour to discuss one of the most fundamental principles of rental-property investing: the risk vs. reward spectrum. Finally, we'll finish by showing a way to safeguard you from yourself and start to get traction on becoming serious about making real estate investing a reality.

THE FIRST STEP—BE FRANK WITH YOURSELF AND DECIDE WHAT YOU WANT

In order to get something, we must forfeit something else. For instance, if your goal was to get a new laptop computer, you would have to pay for it. But there is more than the monetary cost. You'll have to do some research and spend at least a little time trying to find your new computer. What about the work you do to save up the money to buy it? Everything's got a price. Sometimes it's not even monetary, and investing is no exception. There are three resources at our disposal at any one time:

- Money
- Time and Effort
- Knowledge, Experience, Connections.

Which of the three valuable resources do you have that will incentivize people to work with you? If you don't have any of these, you'll need to get to work on at least one of them to be able to provide some value.

Most of us, when thinking about investing, have money and maybe a little bit of time, but no knowledge. That's OK, and will work just fine as long as you are aware of the basics. The following questions will help you understand each of the areas to help identify which resources you can leverage towards building a portfolio.

http://elevateequity.org/what-resources-do-you-have-for-investing

Another important factor is this: why is this journey so important to you? What are you searching for? We understand you want financial freedom, but what will you do with this? This could be anything from traveling the world to volunteering locally for months or even staying home and reading, cooking, catching up on projects or anything that you've always wanted to do.

Go ahead, turn on some music, go outside, take a shower (maybe not at the same time) and put on some reflective music. If you like to journal or are still stuck, think back to the times in which you really felt happy or got into that "flow" state where everything else around you disappeared. What were you doing then? Perhaps whatever you were engaged in then in moments like this can give you insight into what really makes you tick and draws you into your full potential.

Before investing in real estate, I was paralyzed before I finally bought my first property. I realized listening and reading what other people thought was holding me back. Their opinions just didn't resonate with me. *I confused reading for action.* Once I understood myself better, I knew what I wanted. With my end "product" or "experience" in mind, I was able to execute quickly.

We encourage you to begin thinking about high-level goals for yourself, even if it is only one rental this year. More of that will be coming later and will contribute greatly to your success going forward.

RISK VS. REWARD

There is a standard maxim of investing so broad it even applies here: *An investment with a high level of risk also carries a higher reward.* Subsequently, a lower risk "bet" will provide a lower return on your money. This has parallels even in the stock and bond markets. Huge companies usually don't fluctuate wildly in financials because they are established and have a strong track record and large valuations. By comparison, smaller businesses are more unpredictable without the recognition and track record more established companies do.

The same is true with real estate investing. There is a spectrum of risk and reward that correlate well with one another. Here's an example. You have the opportunity to purchase a house in a rough part of town. Because this is an area where most people are not homeowners, are transient and where attitudes of survivalism rules rather than cohesion and trust, home prices are low. There is not much competition to purchase in this area, so the demand is low while the inventory stays constant.

When you buy in these areas, with a low purchase price, the numbers look fantastic. You can buy properties in these areas for $40k or even less, depending on which markets you are looking for. Rent can range from $600–$750 per month, which seem like fantastic numbers. Good luck collecting these rents and repairing property when your place is trashed. Those living there are trying to survive and when push comes to shove, they're not concerned about your property, only themselves.

At the other end of the spectrum, a mansion in the nicest part of town would be relatively low risk because of high demand. Unfortunately, you probably paid too much to make a meaningful return operating it. This approach is better suited for flippers, but that's not us because we are trying to make money passively with little marginal effort. In this scenario, the cash you placed into the property is more secure because resale is more likely to happen. You'll have no issue getting the place rented, but the returns, relative to what you paid for the investment, might not make sense. In that case, you could be getting a better return with a different investment vehicle.

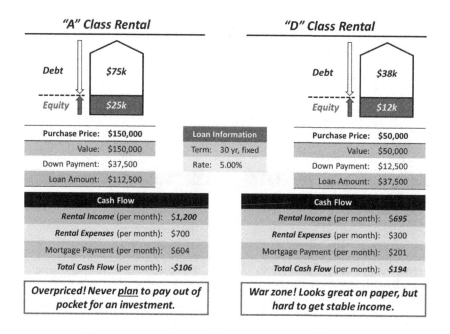

Figure 15

Take a look at Figure 15, which explains what happens when we pursue these extremes on the ends of the spectrum. As buy-and-hold investors, we target our investing in C and B areas (Figure 16), with little hints and indicators pointing in the direction that the areas are improving as demand for people to live there increases. So the question is where do you want to fall on this spectrum?

Are you interested in preserving your capital with lower returns for appreciation growth or would you like to take a more aggressive stance and get increased returns and cash flow for your outlay? Both C and B properties have the opportunity to grow in income and value as well. It's just a matter of the gray area between the extremes. We will discuss more about what makes properties and areas an "A" or a "C" later in Chapter 8. For now, just understand it as a simple building quality grade.

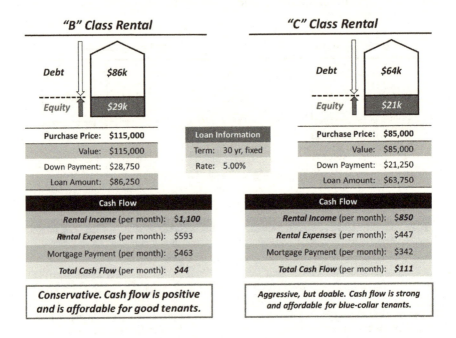

Figure 16

Are you aggressive? Are you willing to take on a bit of stress and potential problems to maximize your returns on your portfolio? Are you content with digging into a market for cheap to modest properties and wait for the area to improve? Or do you want something already in an area that will take care of itself more or less? You have to ask yourself these questions early on, because tackling this now will be one of your leading guides in deciding to purchase when the opportunity presents itself. We've created a quiz to help you decide if you are a cash-flow investor or an appreciation investor.

http://elevateequity.org/what-is-my-risk-tolerance

Take a moment to assess yourself and be honest. If you ha
score, you have a high tolerance and should be a little more ag
in your approach to obtaining properties, down to the lending you
undertake and opportunities you'll explore. If you score low, you may
consider starting with higher-priced properties or stay on the low risk /
low return side of the spectrum until you sharpen your skills to develop
the savvy and the desire to seek higher returns.

PROTECTING YOURSELF FROM....YOU!

Now that we've assessed the risk you're willing to take, we have to be confident in our decision. Here we will spell out some ways to protect yourself from major issues that come up when starting anything new. I know this from personal experience.

PROCRASTINATION

When first starting out, we have wonderful intentions, but life gets in the way. We put things off, and ultimately forget about what we had set out to do. Successful people do things right away, and procrastinators put it off "till tomorrow" which becomes tomorrow's tomorrow and before you know it, it's gone. Some tips to keep procrastination at bay include setting up reminders for yourself (like taping a reminder to the bathroom mirror), declaring your goals publicly on social media, or setting the right goals to do something small each day until it becomes a habit. Other tips include getting organized by making a list of your tasks and taking action on them in the same physical space at the same time everyday. Something simple like asking yourself why you are procrastinating can even help you help yourself. Realizing that you are procrastinating is the first step. There are plenty of resources out there to help you with this that I won't get into here.

took me over a year to finally pull the trigger ...urney, even though what I needed to learn was ...he first month or two. Although I was taking action ... much as I could, I mistook constant learning and readi... ...sitive forward action. While it's good up to a point, there is a law of diminishing returns that begins to destroy the value you are getting from your time. I eventually understood the objective of my first investment was not to make a million dollars, but learn something worthwhile and get in the game in order to be able to talk intelligently with other investors. Another tip for conquering analysis paralysis is to get out and talk to other investors. Surround yourself with people who are doing it. This will help put your experience in perspective to others and you'll start to feel a sense of "peer pressure" to get rolling with an investment of your own.

CONTROL AND FEAR

Making that first real estate investment is often scary since it involves a significant amount of money, not to mention time and energy. You are committing money into something you might have never done before but only seen it work in books or with others. Doing it yourself is very different. In my experiences, I've learned fear is a mostly useless emotion when looking at investments. It means somewhere inside you, there is a lack of confidence or trust. These thoughts don't deserve to take up that space. As your knowledge and experience grow this fear will diminish.

There are usually two types of people: those who freeze in the face of fear and those who take action. Understand that fear means you are testing the boundaries of your comfort zone otherwise known as "growth." Nothing worthwhile was obtained from a place of comfort and ease.

You'll be doing the work of overcoming your fears to learn what your capacity is. Some tips for conquering fear are: keep things in perspective. Ask yourself: "what is the worst thing that can happen?" Often, it's not as bad as you think and you wind up wasting energy worrying. Another approach is to seek advice and tell an experienced investor about what scares you and if it is a reasonable concern.

Taking action and understanding the process and why we are doing this is important. Staying the path and getting out of our own way ensures we will be successful. Bringing a bit of self-awareness into the picture to remove the roadblocks will lead to winning. In the next chapter, we'll take a look at what this looks like, day-to-day as a part-time real estate investor.

ACTION STEPS

➢ Think back to the disadvantages (Chapter 4) of real estate investing to the direct and the indirect benefits (Chapter 3). Without looking back at the chapters, what are the pro's and con's for buy-and-hold real estate investing? Fill out the chart as best you can off memory:

PRO's	CON's
_____	_____
_____	_____
_____	_____
_____	_____
_____	_____
_____	_____
_____	_____

➢ Let's revisit why real estate investing is important to you. Why are you going through all this effort? If it's passive income, what's behind that? What will you do with all the time, money and freedom that real estate investing can provide you?

_____
_____
_____
_____
_____

➤ What resistance, roadblocks or tendencies do you think you'll need to overcome in yourself? Where did you relate or feel emotion as you were reading in the previous chapters?

_____

_____

_____

_____

_____

➤ How will you overcome these tendencies?

_____

_____

_____

_____

_____

CHAPTER 5

THE PART TIME REI MINDSET

"You can't have a million dollar dream with a minimum wage work ethic." —Stephen Hogan

IN ROBERT KIYOSAKI'S classic bestseller, "Rich Dad Poor Dad", he famously talks about the cashflow quadrant. This book inspired me to think outside the box and made me realize there are different ways of earning money other than my job. In the book, Kiyosaki explains how people, who eventually learn to become financially independent, go on a journey from being an "E" (employee) or an "S" (self-employed) to a "B" (business owner) and eventually an "I" (investor). Your mindset changes throughout each phase as you become a full-time investor on the right side of the "Cashflow Quadrant." On the left side of the equation, you are simply someone trading the most precious asset / resource you have, *your time*, for money. See Figure 17 for a visual representation of the Cashflow Quadrant. For those who have not read this life-changing book, you must. Countless others, including myself, were enlightened by how life can be different when income flows in from different sources.

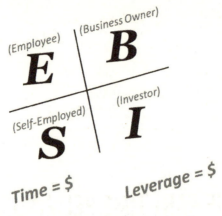

Credits: "Cash Flow Quadrant" by Robert Kiyosaki

Figure 17

After starting my journey as a real estate investor and business owner, I've learned much about these different streams of income. We must strive to have most of our dollars flowing into our pockets from the right side of the cashflow quadrant (the "B" and "I" forms) as opposed to what we have now—trading time for money (the "E" and "S" forms). To make the shift, it has to be step by step, starting with ourselves inside our mind and manifesting outwards. True change begins when we commit to a decision and attract thoughts, concepts and people into our life, at which point manifestation in the outside world begins. Our education, our mindset and our determination are key aspects to this. To help this journey, I'd like to share problems I encountered and then conquered in order to keep going despite the temptation to quit moving from the left side to the right side.

EXPECTATIONS

One day, I looked at a cleaning and maintenance turnover bill after a tenant vacated our property and told my wife "I don't think this is working. I'm not happy doing this and we don't have enough to pay this bill in our bank account. What have we done? Did we make a mistake?"

She reassured me that we both knew things were not going according to plan and we had set our expectations too high from our previous experiences, resulting in needless suffering.

In a similar case, I set up my parents with rental property and made the mistake of not talking through their expectations on risk vs. reward. Eventually, the properties stabilized, but put unnecessary strain on them by not level-setting on expectations.

Despite all of the positive things that a stabilized portfolio can give you, a healthy detachment from property performance on a month-by-month basis will reduce stress and increase the likelihood of continued expansion.

If you expect the first property you buy to make a million dollars, you will be severely disappointed and will likely not have the fortitude to continue your journey when a setback occurs (and it will). This is the opposite of what we are trying to do. Rather, the healthiest approach is to shift your attention from trying to make an infinite cash-on-cash return from day 1 to *learning and gaining experience*. While it may seem backwards, trying to find the perfect investment can lead to analysis paralysis.

Instead, trust yourself and acquire your first property with the intent of learning something. This will net you more returns quicker because you actually took action and learned your lessons. You simply don't know what you don't know.

Real legacy wealth is built over time and not "quick flipped" like shows on HGTV. If you prepare and gather ingredients well, understand the recipe in a general sense, and give it enough time to cook, the result will almost always be delicious. Do not expect to be a millionaire overnight without any effort on your part. This is a fool's errand. It will take understanding, time, effort and money. You will eventually get the hang of it and start to want to take on more. A funny thing happens as you understand that you've put limitations on yourself and discover that *you* are the obstacle, nothing more.

Remember: long-term holds, with all things considered and given our situation as part-time real estate investors, almost always perform better than repeated short-term flips or wholesale deals. Flippers who end up creating a pipeline of flips and manage a business, find that doing this becomes their full-time job and tax rules are not as advantageous. Often, I hear these flippers say, "I wish I had held on to a few of those. They've doubled in value in the last five years." This is where we want to be. Stay long-term focused and continue to grow your stack of LEGO blocks.

MISTAKES = LEARNING

This may sound backwards, but I started to really take off in my business when I changed my perspective from trying to succeed every time to actually trying to fail. This worked because of my personality. Because I was so strongly tied to trying to find every conceivable advantage in every situation, I stopped trusting myself.

Once I understood that about 80% of my criteria was met, it was time to act. I was coming from a place where if the 20% that was not as important as my "must haves" was not there, it was a failure. *So, I started to seek out failure.* You heard me right, I wanted to make mistakes, because I found what held me back from closing on a property can be renegotiated, rectified, or made insignificant by using creativity. If risk materialized, I dealt with it. Even though it was still painful, I was glad to go through it because, again, it taught me something. I would not make the same mistake again. Warren Buffet, the most successful stock investor of all time, says knowledge and education in yourself is the best investment you can ever make because it will never go down in value.

Failure and mistakes are temporary. Making a mistake once happens to everyone, and regardless of the size, you can, and will, recover. Lessons also tend to compound themselves, and paired up with best practices you've learned, give a comprehensive understanding of your craft.

As you take your lumps in investing, you'll slowly see a bigger picture. The pain you go through is a reminder that there is risk you signed up for, and with risk, there is bound to be reward. Some of the best lessons I've learned are mistakes I walked into blindly, completely unaware of the terrible consequences that might play out if I kept going. This taught me so much and pushed the bounds of what I thought I was capable of doing. Making mistakes helps us understand where the edges of our knowledge and mindset are, and points the way to pushing those edges out. This makes us more valuable and experienced. The actual habit of stepping into the unknown when you are not comfortable allows us to grow quickly. It pounds knowledge into our brains faster than learning from books or podcasts.

NEVER IRREVERSIBLE

Experiencing discomfort is a vital part of the learning process in real estate investing. While that is true, remember that you have options in almost every situation. Not every option is great but they are there, and you are free to choose what's best for you. If a rental or an investment is not going the way you expected, or you're going through something in your personal life that demands too much time or energy, you may have nothing left to devote to your investments. In this case, doing nothing may be an option. At that point it is up to your team to step in and address issues for you. Selling is also an option, but time and money are counterbalanced, so if you want top dollar to dump a headache of a property, you will need to wait for the right buyer. Inversely, it can be gone quickly if you are willing to lose a potentially significant portion of your investment stake.

When you become fully immersed in investing and start to get a decent-sized portfolio under your belt (from one to three properties or investments), you develop faith and confidence in yourself because you see evidence of your plan working. Your LEGO blocks materialize and you see tangible results. This is gold. Once you taste that success, you ask yourself, "Boy, that wasn't too hard—this is kind of fun. When's the next one coming?" This is the point where you realize you have made it over the hill and are now leveraging that effort and experience, making it work for you. In addition, the full-time job is supporting you financially while you build your escape ladder with the dollars earned there. This faith in yourself is what we depend on when times get tough or you are presented with an opportunity.

POSITIVITY BREEDS SUCCESS

Positivity is the most important aspect of someone who successfully invests in real estate or runs any meaningful business over the long term. Staying positive gives you a mental edge and toughness that allows you to keep coming back for more despite any and all difficulties.

Being patient and positive with yourself gives you space to think creatively and focus on solving a particular problem, while having faith that a solution exists in the face of mounting issues or costs. Give yourself a chance to breathe, tap into your faith and determine the best option to solve the problem. This will be a common skill that will accompany you throughout most of your journey and will be useful to nearly any situation that life throws at you.

Being positive has amazing benefits on your health, relationships, spirituality, career, and your investing. Positive people live longer, make better decisions, are less stressed, receive more external support, and persevere under sustained difficult situations that lead them to success.[11] Some of the most successful people in the world (W. Clement Stone, Jim Carrey, Oprah Winfrey, Norman Vincent Peele, and others) attribute their success to never-ending positivity and faith in themselves.

---

11 http://www.jongordon.com/positive-tip-11-benefits.html

Take stock in the fact that you have picked up this book and have begun exploring a way to better your life through financial independence and adding valuable marketplace tools and skills to your toolbelt. Celebrate and congratulate yourself for this. If you would like to explore more about this, there are numerous resources you can pursue to increase your positive energy or to be aware of your negative self-talk. Later, in Chapter 9, we'll provide some tools to help build your positive energy to propel and lift you through any difficulties in your personal, professional, and investing situations.

These are basic mental jiu-jitsu skills that underpins my success as a real estate buy-and-hold investor that served me well while holding a full-time job. Although your "game-changing" lessons may be different from mine, this is the beauty of starting and running a business with real estate investing—we can all learn from each other. What skills will you need to invest in real estate that you already possess? What do you think you will need to learn about yourself, or what, if you had to identify one thing, is holding you back from investing? Knowing the answer to these questions could help unlock a part of yourself that's ready to take off like a rocket ship!

Now that we've gotten ourselves in line, we'll be taking it to the next level. Our mission now is to get our biggest ally on board our rocket ship to success—our partners.

ACTION STEPS

➢ Think back to a time in which you took the time and effort to learn a new skill or something that requires time for practice. Examples are learning to play pool, basketball, baseball, or learn a language.

➢ What did you do to learn this? How much time and energy did it take you to get as far as you are today?

_____

_____

_____

_____

_____

➢ What did you do to overcome and persevere through temptation to quit?

_____

_____

_____

_____

_____

CHAPTER 6

GETTING THE OTHER HALF ON BOARD

"One plus one, doesn't equal two. It becomes the power of eleven." —Mark Victor Hansen

IF YOU DON'T have a spouse, significant other or partner in your life now, please consider this chapter optional. It may be handy if, and when, that situation changes for you. If you do, however, share financial responsibilities with someone else, do not overlook this chapter. It can preserve the domestic tranquility on the home front and help prevent unpleasant disagreements.

When I speak about investing in real estate, many fail to include their significant others into the decision-making and learning process. I know from personal experience that if your teammate at home is not included in your investing, especially in the beginning, you may experience difficulty getting on the same page. The "why's" must be aligned, because going into this business, or any business for that matter, takes sacrifices some may not immediately understand, start to fear, or promote increasing resentment.

Including your partner throughout the process of investing from intention to execution will yield many benefits to both parties. Let's take a look at what I've found to be true in my relationship with my spouse and what you may find as well.

COMMUNICATION AND SHARED DISCOVERY

If you bring your partner with you, he/she will challenge you with questions. They will ask, "why are we going through all this effort?" or "how does this help us?" These, as well as other questions, are worth thinking about and justifying. This process has an extra benefit of increasing communication between the both of you, as if exploring and going on another journey together. This will only increase your connectedness, trust, harmony and understanding within your partnership.

Key aspects to consider when talking about real estate investing are to keep things at the 3,000 foot perspective and take it slowly. Using language such as "we" instead of "I" will help invite inclusion. Ask yourselves, how will you both decide to handle the profits, or more importantly, if a property portfolio goes into a deficit, how will you make this work, given the situation you're in now? It's important to have someone on board who will understand profits should not be abused. You will need to have someone supporting you when things go wrong, rather than blame you and cause more stress.

These problem-solving conversations may even open yourself and partner up to learn more about your own decision-making processes and priorities, as individuals and as a couple. The conversation should be kept within the framework of high-level basic concepts to push and pull you through your investing. I recommend estimating your partner's risk tolerance, what's important to them, and what you think they would be willing to sacrifice to make what they want materialize.

SHARED GOALS AND PURPOSE

When you start the conversation with your partner about this, ask questions and stay open minded. Start with what they would do if they didn't have to worry about money and help them visualize what it would be like, trying not to project too much of your own visions onto their own. Listen for keywords as they speak and what's important to them. Ask what they think it would take to make it happen and if they would be willing to work towards making it a reality. At this point, it's important to share your own vision as well, understanding that the word "us" is the word that should be used 99 times to each "I."

Try to get a clear picture of what you both are working towards and how you would like to explore something different to make the shared vision a reality. This should be something that compels you both to push on, and will be a reminder about why you are working so hard. Your partner (and even you) may end up learning a lot about yourselves and start to connect on a deeper level as you gain more insights as to what makes each other tick. In some cases, you may discover it may not be the right time to start your real estate investing career. That's ok, too.

INVOLVING YOUR PARTNER IN THE COSTS

It's imperative to be open about what you know and do not know. When I skipped this advice it put a bit of strain on us because we both thought I knew what I was doing. My spouse trusted me, and I misplaced my confidence in a property we purchased out of state, thinking it would be easy to handle. The consequences led to me getting into something I was not ready for. And, it cost me quite a bit of time, money, energy, comfort and stress.

Not informing your partner about potential costs of time, money, energy, stress, and outside appearances can prematurely end your investing before it really gets a chance to begin. You've got to share all possible pitfalls with your partner, and be ready to explain what you're doing each step of the way. Real estate investing touches on all of the finite resources people have, and if your partner is not with you, along with understanding what you're trying to do, they could feel there is less of you to go around. Deep resentment and anger could be a consequence.

BALANCING IT ALL OUT

When we start investing, we may inadvertently give ourselves permission to spend as much time, money, or resources available to make it happen. While this is true, we have to remember that we are still human beings. Being in a relationship helps you remember to stay balanced. When you're in balance, things come your way and you're more effective with your time. This is much better than when you're putting yourself and your relationships under self-imposed stress. Doing that will only reduce your effectiveness. Much like trying to throw a glass of water onto a burning building won't achieve much, working on your portfolio without being rested and motivated won't get better results. Within the context of a relationship, compromises and trade offs are essential.

With my marriage, I was focused on building a portfolio of properties so we as a couple and family would be able to enjoy as much time together as possible. The reality, though, manifested in confusion and frustration for my wife. We found that I was devoting so much of my energy to real estate investing that she felt like she wasn't needed. She abruptly told me if I didn't make changes in communication and priorities, the future I was trying to build for us might vanish. This was a huge reality check, and made me question how important this was and what we were willing to sacrifice to make our vision come true.

SOME MYTHS ABOUT INVESTING TO SHARE

There are basic myths that I'd like to take a moment to dispel, in case they come up in your conversations with your partner or within yourself. These myths are related to our valuable time and energy resources.

MYTH: INVESTING WILL LEAD TO LOSS OF SECURITY

In most relationships, or single individual financial planning, there is a compelling need to save cash and keep a nice "pad" in the bank for a rainy day. This is sound advice and I agree 100% with this. You should not be using your life savings in any investment you are not yet knowledgeable about or don't have a trusted network to help. No one is forcing you to do anything and you can underwrite or commit as much as you are willing to, as long as you keep your family well-positioned in the case of an emergency..

MYTH: INVESTING IS TOO HARD TO LEARN

Obviously, you have picked up this book. I can guarantee it's not hard to learn, unless you let it be. Your mindset should be your guiding principle, backed by basic knowledge. It comes down to your own expectations and taking action.

MYTH: IT'S BETTER TO STAY IN THE STOCK MARKET

Do I have to go here? See Chapter 2 if you need a refresher.

MYTH: IT TAKES TOO MUCH MONEY AND TIME TO INVEST

This is also untrue. While having more resources on either of these does make entry into real estate investing much more fruitful and easier, it is not required. There are ways to team with others, partner with your retirement accounts, use hard money, or more. We will go more in-depth in coming chapters as we cover how investing works.

MYTH: TENANTS AND CLOGGED TOILETS AT 1 AM

Nope, not true. This is why we hire property managers who handle this directly. Your tenants won't even know your name or address unless they make a concerted effort to track you down.

Only you know what is best for you and your partner and how to approach them about investing. Your goal is to inform, inspire, and lead both of you through the process of obtaining your first investment, and how you decide to go there can only be determined by you. Please *do not put this off until after* you close on your first property. While it may be a great thing for your bottom line and for your experience, what point does it serve if you've abused trust with your partner? It is essential to listen and understand their feelings and know where they are coming from. Look forward to this conversation as the start of something deeper and more meaningful on many levels. You both deserve it.

After explaining expectations on the home front, it's time to turn to what will actually make it work for us as busy professionals. In the next chapter, we'll explore techniques and tools to help you prepare to create the mental and physical space in which you will need to start your investing while working.

ACTION STEPS

- If you have a significant other and have not been talking about real estate investing yet, it is time to loop them in. Start by gauging their interest first during your daily interactions by asking them what they think about investing in real estate.

- Engage in an exercise to think about what's important to you both and where you'd like to go as a couple. Propose a time and space where you are uninterrupted and able to freely talk without being distracted or tired. Write down when this will be and where:

  Date: _____, Time from: _____
  to: _____ At (location): _____

  This is a good time and place free from distractions like:

  _____

- Don't push or try to convince. State why you'd like to consider investing in real estate and listen. Be sure to use the word "we" as much as you can and avoid pointing blame, pointing mainly to the future. Remember that investing in any area is a risk that involves you both since it's tied to your personal finances, time and energy.

- If the answer you get is "no" or you sense resistance, stop and ask questions to try to learn more about your significant others' fears. Are they valid?

- Understand that if you get a "no" now, it's based on a fear or belief guided by false information or an unfounded feeling. Know that a "no" now is not necessarily a "no" permanently. Addressing and clarifying deeper into that "no" is a good thing because it exposes the limits of our knowledge and gaps in communication. It will also strengthen the overall trust in the relationship.

➢ In your opinion, how did this conversation go? Make some notes here:

1) What common ground were you able to find?
   _____
   _____

2) What did you hear was important to your significant other that you didn't know?
   _____
   _____

3) In your opinion, how did this first conversation go?
   _____
   _____

4) What emotion was present in the dialogue (anger, apathy, fear, etc.)? Why do you think those emotions came out?
   _____
   _____

5) What further steps or communication, if at all, are needed?
   _____
   _____

CHAPTER 7

THE TOOLS AND PROCESSES OF THE SUCCESSFUL PART-TIME RE INVESTOR

"If you are not willing to risk the usual, you will have to settle for the ordinary." —Jim Rohn

NOW, ARMED WITH the right mindset and proper expectations we're ready to equip ourselves with tools to help pull this together. This chapter has more of a practical feel to help wrap your head around the one lingering question: "How am I going to be able to do this while working? I'm so busy I don't even have time for myself..." The truth is that *most people overestimate what they can do in one day and underestimate what they can accomplish in one year.*

There are tools you can implement to help you work smarter without the need for working harder.

SETTING THE STAGE

First, consider what you will be giving up to pursue investing in real estate on the side. Consider our discussion from Chapter 4 again. In most cases, it will be time, energy, money and risk—so how flexible are you in each of these areas? If you haven't taken this assessment or don't have a strong feel for this, now is the time to do so.

http://elevateequity.org/what-resources-do-you-have-for-investing

Consistency and taking action are the elements linked to success. Remember from Chapter 5 that lessons learned tend to compound on each other. This is also true with success because as long as you are moving the needle covering a reasonable amount of time, in a year or more, you are making progress. Soon, I'll be asking you to review your goals and break them down into weekly and daily actions. Despite any enthusiasm you may have, you've got to set goals that stretch you beyond your comfort zone. We're looking to establish a new habit, and that grows best when it doesn't take a monumental effort on your end.

Here's the secret I stumbled onto while working full time: taking action "no matter what" diminishes the effort over time as you grow your holdings. See Figure 18 for a visual of this concept.

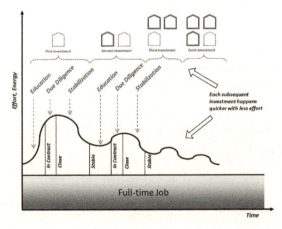

Figure 18

When you first start out, it's a blank canvas so your level of effort is simply curiousity or driven by book knowledge. As time goes on, you gain a slight familiarity with your investment approach and become overwhelmed with choices, possibilities and the unknown. You understand how much you don't know and begin to execute. The effort, at this point, is significant on your first properties. After that, the effort dramatically diminishes since you're now familiar with the process. With each property, or investment, you add to your portfolio, your experience increases and soon you are investing with almost no effort on your part.

The most dangerous aspect of this curve is when effort peaks, and potential investors can't see the benefits due to the difficulties. The work and knowledge gap seems like trying to climb Everest. Trust you will reach the summit and make it "over the hill" to enjoy and celebrate your downhill coasting. Funny enough, after obtaining a few properties, you may let your guard down and start to take your hands off the wheel, not doing due diligence, being too optimistic, or over-extending criteria to force making something work.

Both Dave Ramsey and Warren Buffet refer to snowballs when building wealth or skill sets (refer to the Resources Section of our website for more details). A snowball, when rolled down a hill, starts slowly and picks up a bit of snow at first. The accumulated snow starts picking up more snow each time it rolls over. Then it starts to pick up speed until it becomes a boulder and contains enough power to cause an avalanche (Figure 19).

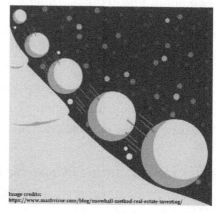

Figure 19

We definitely want to harness this power, but we also need to set our snowball on the right hill at the right speed. Let's take a look at some ways in which we can consistently and methodically set up our snowfield for our snowballs.

SYSTEMS AND PROCESSES

Here we will cover tools I've used to understand real estate investing, starting with single-family homes and gradually moving to multifamily investing. While some tools may resonate with you right away and others may not seem to make sense, I encourage you to at least consider them. Those you do select, try to implement right away. It will be hard to see what results you'll be able to achieve with consistency, but these all worked for me in various ways to help me break through and achieve my goals.

TIME BLOCKING

Starting out, this is one of the most important things you can do for yourself. Pick an appropriate block of time that you're willing to devote in building your portfolio, however much that is. It can be anything from 30 minutes up to an hour or more each day. I personally schedule two hours, one in the morning from 7 am–8 am at the office before most people get in. Most days, I'm able to block out an additional hour for lunch to work on my investments or education.

Place that block of time on your calendar. Even if you don't have anything on your mind during this period or have no idea what you'll be doing, use the time to plan out what activities seem in alignment with your goals.

Jerry Seinfeld, the prolific standup comic and sitcom star, claims that his success came from consistent work day-to-day. He had a simple calendar posted in a very visible place and started out crossing out days on it each day that he stuck to his one hour of joke writing. After a while, he claimed that he became personally invested in the long chain he had maintained. The simple act of not wanting to break the chain kept him focused on how he was spending the time to focus on the goals. This is a useful technique we can adopt as well.

REMINDERS, ALERTS, AND CHECKLISTS

Even well-intentioned part-time investors may forget or be tempted to skip their block of time to devote to our success each day. By leveraging electronic tools with alerts and checklists, you can help keep yourself accountable. Set up a reminder on your phone or desktop to alert you that this time you're promised yourself is a priority. We want to set ourselves up for success now while the intention and motivation is fresh. By setting alarms and reminders ahead of time, we are making it slightly harder for us to veer off our path of devoting the time we need to set aside to succeed.

If you're looking for tools to use to help you with this, I've compiled a list of my favorite electronic and not-so-electronic tools in the resources section of my website to keep you on track. I've even built out a customizable schedule with all the activities needed to achieve success in a short time in my Resource sections of my website.

FEAR-SETTING

This term, as made popular by Tim Ferriss involves the practice of taking what you are afraid of, either consciously or unconsciously, and putting it to paper. It helps you to place the worst-case scenarios you fear right in front of you. It then helps you untangle the emotional connection you carry with it and transform it into a plan of action. As Tim Ferriss alludes to in his podcast and on his blog, this important exercise has preceded many of his largest successes in the past. You can find more about this in the Book Resources Section of our website.

In my experience, many of my biggest wins in the past were right outside of my comfort zone. If you can confront your fears and break them down, removing the emotion from them, you will grow as a person. Your fear dissolves, capacity expands and confidence increases as you move past the limitations you place on yourself. It's true that the source of these fears are, for the most part, a story that we tell ourselves and needlessly believe.

THE ONE THING

In "The One Thing," authors Gary Keller and Jay Papasan expand on the importance of consistent action on your No. 1 priority and using your time blocks for your One Thing. There are some excellent tools in this book to help select what your focus should be as well as providing persuasive and motivating arguments to know your One Thing and stick to your time blocks.

One effective tool in the book that stood out to me was the idea of dominoes, lined up in a path, can knock over the next domino slightly less than twice its size. Each domino in sequence is a unit of effort and, if lined up and allowed to go far enough, has the power to topple an elephant or skyscraper. Think of your repeated efforts in taking action consistently as your dominoes.

CAREFULLY SELECTED GOALS AND DEADLINES

If you haven't yet created a vision and drawn yourself fully into it, now is the time to do so. It doesn't have to be specific, but it does have to act like a compass to direct the setting of your goals and the deadlines you'll be giving yourself. The next step is to break down your vision into components or large goals, whatever this means for you. Ideally this is one that you suspect may take a year or more. Grab a pen and paper, and at the top of the page, write down your vision.

If you are more visual, feel free to create a vision "board." As an example, my vision board from Q4 last year can be found in Figure 20.

Figure 20

You can even do a vision "video." Check out the Mind Movie video I made for myself here for an idea of what that could look like.

http://elevateequity.org/the-book/my-mind-movie/

The point is to create something that will compel you to succeed and what your life will be like when you have freed yourself from the rat race.

From there, outline one or more large goals to help achieve this vision. If this is a goal you can accomplish in one year, double it. In Grant Cardone's book, "The 10X Rule: The Only Difference Between Success and Failure," he talks about the process of taking what he thinks is doable in one year and multiplying it by 10 to see what you are really made of. His reasoning: even if you miss your goal by 50%, you still have managed to do 4-5 times better than you thought you would. So, be brave and courageous. You are capable of so much more than you think. You will then realize quickly that your fear, rather than a perceived knowledge or experience gap, will be the only thing holding you back.

Break down your annual goals into what you would need to do on a monthly, weekly, and daily basis. Always work within the realm of setting goals within your control, using Figure 21 as a template. For example, if your monthly goal is to get into a purchase contract with two properties per month, this is unrealistic because it's dependent on another party (a seller and broker or agent) to act. A more appropriate goal would be to analyze 40 properties per month. This is something fully in your realm of control.

Figure 21

After completing this, apart from feeling pretty good about your own future, you should have a much more organized and thought-out plan of attack on what to do with your time to self-educate and get your first dollar of equity to work.

USING YOUR ZERO-TIME

When referring to "zero-time," I am referring to all the gaps in time in which we spend amounting to dead space, without productivity, throughout our day. Examples of this include your drive time to work, standing in line, waiting for an appointment, grocery shopping, taking a break for a walk outside, or repetitive workouts such as running or following your routine.

By simply having podcasts shows lined up in advance that interest you in real estate investing, finance, or personal growth, you can, with a simple finger press on your screen, listen to valuable content on your mobile device. This makes you even more productive during times that will come to you inevitably. A list of my personal podcast lineup and other recommendations can also be found in the resources section of my website. Subscribe to these podcasts and start up the habit of understanding when zero-time hits you unexpectedly. Soon, it'll become second nature.

Over the years, I've become a master at this much to my wife's chagrin, keeping myself surrounded all the time by educational podcasts. This multiplies my knowledge over a long period of time that will be leveraged in many ways. I even went so far as to buy a bluetooth shower head (and yes, they make those) to listen to my podcasts in the bathroom and shower.

POSTING AND VISUAL REMINDERS

Our world is what we perceive it to be. If we view negative content and immerse ourselves in conversations that make us feel smaller or don't compel us to expand, we will start to internalize this limiting feedback if exposed day after day. It may then become our reality. Messages enter our minds subconsciously and subliminally, so surrounding ourselves with positive imagery repeatedly will start to shape our attitude. Jim Rohn, the great motivational speaker and success coach was known for saying that "you are the average of the five people you hang around the most." Influences come at us from every direction and we owe it to ourselves to be the gatekeeper.

By posting positive messages and goals, *everywhere*, we will be surrounded and lifted up with what we are working towards. You can:

- Take a picture of your goals and have it as the background / lock screen for your phone.
- Copy your vision and goals and tape them to your mirror / bathroom door so you see them every day.
- If you carry a wallet, write a note and place it there so you see it every time you open it.
- Set a reminder on your phone or use an app to be reminded of your goals.
- Write a post-dated check to yourself in the amount of $1 million and secure it to your bathroom mirror where you can see it every day.

Doing this will force your goals deeper into your subconscious, and throughout the day, you'll think more about your goals, instead of the negative thoughts that would have otherwise been there. It takes time, but doing this outside-in type of work really will help keep your head and thoughts aligned with your vision and will remind you if (and when) you might forget them.

GET A MENTOR

One of the fastest ways to get where you want to go is to talk to someone who is a few steps further along on the path. There are plenty of people, courses, and "gurus" out there who can help you reach your goals for a sizable fee, and many of them are listed in our Resources section found in Chapter 9. We have resources and coaching available for you on our website as well. This book is a great start already, so keep going. A mentor will help you from wasting time on things that aren't important so that you can keep yourself making swift progress. It is almost always better to seek help with any issue in which you are not experienced.

ACCOUNTABILITY AND PUNISHMENTS

My favorite technique to maintain focus on your goals and moving in the right direction is to find someone who is either on the journey with you, or are interested in what you are doing (which can, oftentimes, be your partner or a good friend). You'll want to select someone that is dependable and will hold up their end of the bargain, too.

You can start by sharing your goals, and determining a *regular* meeting time (twice a month, or weekly, whatever works for you) where you share your progress and whether you have hit the goals you've established. An agenda is not necessary when starting out, but should be treated like a check-in meeting. The meetings don't have to be long and may feel strange at first. If that's the case, consider it more like a gym buddy arrangement in which you motivate each other to show up and work out. After all, this is the agreement you've made with this other person.

In the space below, indicate who you think would make an excellent accountability partner and make it a small goal to reach out and explain what you're doing. Be sure to bring a copy of your goals so they can hold you accountable. If they are up for it, ask them to do the same.

My ideal accountability partner is:

_____ (number one choice) or

_____ (number two choice) or

_____ (number three choice).

For the most serious among us, I recommend setting up a punishment for yourself in the scenario that you don't reach or hit your weekly goals. That may include texting a picture of you eating a food that makes you want to throw up. Or, you could write a post-dated check to the political party or non-profit charity that you disagree with most and your partner will cash if you don't act. Another idea would be doing 500 pushups in one "sitting" for as long as it takes. Trust your own judgement on what you think would provide you with an appropriate level of motivation, taking into account what you know about your personality.

LEVERAGING YOURSELF

As an engineer by training, this one came easily to me, but could be tricky for others. Don't sweat this though, because you'll start to do this on any scale that works for you.

When you finish something that takes a lot of time, for example, underwriting a property, create systems for yourself to be able to leverage that work you just went through. In this case, from your first underwriting tool, create a template you can use to speed up underwriting on the next property. Make template-based emails in which you can simply copy and paste if you are interested in making an offer on a property. If you use Zillow or Redfin, take the data that's exported and underwrite everything you filtered on one spreadsheet. If you don't know how to do this, don't worry, you'll find tools that work for you on my website that are being continuously updated.

USING ELECTRONIC TOOLS TO GET WHAT YOU NEED FASTER

I am a huge fan of Google Docs, and use them whenever possible. You can add important items to look at later in Google Drive straight from an email sent to you (if you use Gmail). You can set up reminders, tasks and time blocks to finish an activity at a later date using Google Tasks and Google Calendar, all accessible to you within Gmail and works nicely on the go via smartphone. I love this and wouldn't have been able to keep myself organized enough without it. That is me. If this doesn't resonate with you, that's no problem, but find some way to organize your data and communication to simplify decision making. It's all about ease of access so your energy is spent growing your business versus low-value administration.

I've learned over the last several years not to trust your memory. Whenever you commit something to a seller, partner, buyer or property manager, immediately "time" block it or write it down somewhere while you are still on the phone or hearing the news. You never know when you need to be reminded of something to be done immediately or scheduled later. I personally use Google Tasks that have built in time-based reminders. This habit will help you come across as more professional and a cut above "the average bear."

Use these tools wisely—they could become the foundation of something great. I've listed what's worked for me as I started up. Note that I still use these tools. Because this book is written for hard-working employees and self-employed professionals, I'm assuming the amount of time you have to build your portfolios of real estate equity is minimal. Have faith that if you use a few of these from the onset, it will give you the best possible chance of reaching your goals.

Now we've got our mindset right. Let's go over the basic terminology of real estate investing to build a solid foundation of knowledge and build your portfolio.

ACTION STEPS

- Pick a few podcasts from the resources section of the book to download and subscribe to on your mobile device for your dedicated time block and Zero-time.

- If you haven't already done so, find a regular time block to focus on your real estate investing each day, even if it's only for 30 minutes. Write in your commitment here:

    At _____ o' clock every _____ (Mon-Fri or Mon-Sat), I will focus on real estate investing ONLY for _____ minutes learning and taking action. I will do this at _____ (location) uninterrupted by other distractions.

- What is your primary goal? Think outside of the realm of real estate and more about what real estate can enable or achieve for you.

    Real estate investing will enable me to:
    _____
    _____
    _____

- Find an accountability partner that you share your short and medium-term goals with. Ideally this person has the right personality and interest. Select someone you see most days at home (your significant other) or at the office (a colleague or friend).

➢ What kind of person are you when it comes to large projects that demand consistent action? Do you normally stick to your goals? If so, why? If not, why and what steps can you make to start making those changes?

_____
_____
_____
_____
_____

CHAPTER 8

"FUN"DAMENTALS OF RE INVESTING

"The best investment on Earth is Earth." —Louis Glickman

OK, MAYBE IT'S not all "fun," but this important stuff you'll need to know.

The easiest way to process a new concept is to see a broad overview before diving into the details. This is much like how a captain must know the final destination in order to set the right course. In this chapter, we will cover basic definitions to help build a vocabulary and frame of reference.

Because we are busy professionals, I'll do my best to provide the essential tools for intelligent conversations with other investors or people involved in your acquisition and operations.

MARKETS AND CYCLES

If you've lived in the same area most of your life, you probably understand one part of the country can be totally different than your hometown. While amenities, weather, people, culture, and busy-ness are very different, the dynamics of investing in these markets can vary dramatically. Not only home pricing, but rental laws, lending guidelines, weather-related considerations and construction methods can be completely different. For instance, one market may have cinder block construction in anticipation for hurricanes in certain regions of Florida, while other homes may not be built with AC systems, commonplace in cooler areas like Washington State.

As a real estate investor, it's important to understand all these dynamics, but what's most important, as an investor, is the bottom line—how we are going to make our returns? Some areas are cash-flow markets. These are places where expected rents are high relative to property purchase prices. Others are appreciation markets where rents are small and home prices high.

An example of a cash-flow market would be Cleveland or Kansas City, while an appreciation market would be Seattle or Los Angeles. Coastal cities are generally appreciation markets while midwestern and some southern cities are considered cash-flow markets. What makes an appreciation market different from a cash-flow market is the number of homeowners. This leads to high demand and low supply, because everyone wants to move in. Most homeowners have an innate pride of ownership and sense of community which drives desirability or demand, thus higher prices.

Those fortunate to have a home in such an area will see prices shooting up. In cash-flow markets, jobs are changing, or being added, and the market is dynamic, so people tend to be more transient at the general demographic level. Skilled labor, commanding high salaries, may not be attracted to the area because not enough of these jobs have been created which equates to fewer homeowners. Rents are pegged to what employers can pay, indicative of the current economy.

Appreciation markets are marked by low capitalization rate (or "cap rate" for short). This is a fancy way of measuring how much income to expect for the purchase price you pay. For example, in a coastal (appreciation) market, you can expect capitalization rates to be extremely low. A $1 million dollar house (if you were not living in it) may rent out for $3,000–$3,500 per month, which pencils out to a cap rate of around 2-3% per year.

Conversely, in a cash-flow market, you can typically see much higher cap rates around 7–12%, meaning a $100,000 house would get you around $850–$1,100 per month in rents. Compared to the appreciation market, though, your property value and rents will not climb as fast as they would if they were in an appreciation market (Figure 22).

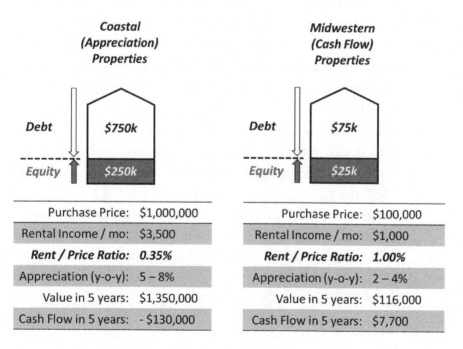

Figure 22

There are many markets with cash flow and appreciation characteristics, indicative of areas that are growing. In any single major metro area market, you have submarkets that also display very different characteristics. Soon you will be able to identify these pockets of "transition." This is key when we discuss acquiring your first dollar in equity in your target markets.

These submarkets are made up of neighborhoods and even streets that can be analyzed at such a granular level. So much to the point that you can see massive wealth and pride of ownership visible on one side of a block and complete disrepair and neglect on the other. Investors communicate this by using a term called a "grade" of an area within a market and properties themselves. Commonly, we refer to an area being a "B area, C property" or a "D area, C property." Here's a short and informal explanation of the grading codes, also depicted in Figure 23:

- A: brand new, luxury finishes and amenities, prime locations near downtown or commercial shopping and entertainment cores, construction completed within the last 20 years.
- B: white-collar resident class, solid quality construction, upgraded amenities, close to transit spots, "renters by choice," reasonable rents, good safety and schools, construction in the last 40 years.
- C: blue-collar resident class, basic finishes and amenities, farther from decent schools and transit systems, aging infrastructure, less access to shopping, construction complete within the last 60-70 years.
- D: transient resident class, "renters by necessity", vacant or run-down property, unsafe or falling apart, health issues and permitting violations, very old construction from 80 years or more.

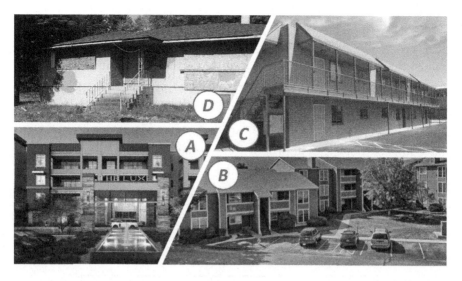

Figure 23

Investors like us are looking for B and C areas and properties.

One other major factor to consider is time. Because the economy moves and pushes jobs, people and economies around at a local and national level, demand for housing is constantly shifting, oftentimes in different directions. real estate markets are driven by the overall economic cycle of booming economies maturing, declining, and recessing into depressions or larger recessions. Local economies feel this effect differently.

Higher value economies in appreciation markets at the coasts command more financial weight due to the large amounts and frequency of transactions from an abundance of employment. When a financial crisis takes hold, high numbers of jobs start to fall away from the economy, causing a ripple effect that trickles outward to housing and other businesses. Think of a tech worker in California who makes $200,000 per year and carries a mortgage balance on their personal residence of $1,200,000. What happens to them when the economy shifts, and they, along with everyone on that street loses their job due to a stock market or currency crash?

Values start to fall quickly and this domino effect continues. In fact, the values continue to fall until the market reaches an "equilibrium" point to adjust to the economic signals that drove it. The end result is significantly lower values due to a sudden oversupply of property and less jobs to support them. Values are then much smaller than when the "trigger" took place. Meanwhile, in the heartland of the US, most homeowners have smaller mortgages in proportion to their salaries and have since paid off their homes, or if they do lose their $100,000 home, this effect is not as significant as one person in CA losing their $1,200,000 home. Figure 24 below helps to explain how this dynamic can be visualized over time for typical single-family house investments.

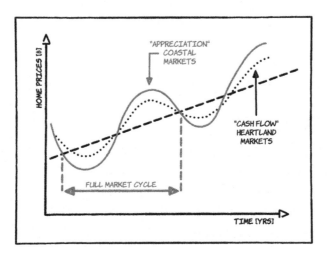

Figure 24

While conventional wisdom confirms this, the last 30 years of data, based on the Case-Shiller Index, shows home prices in the top metro areas appreciate more, and until the turn of the century, lost more value (Figure 25). Market cycles do happen, but their effects are complicated and getting more and more complex in recent years since the 2008 crash and the recent COVID-19 economic fallout. This is an indication that our conventional wisdom and idealized understanding of home prices needs to be approached more cautiously in the real world.

Consider the current Coronavirus pandemic economy. As Nassim Nicholas Taleb points out in his book, "The Black Swan," unforseen "black swan" events shake up the foundations of our otherwise normally functioning systems. While it's good to have a reference point as to what a predictable economy will look like, the best we can do as investors in all assets is to first educate ourselves. This then fosters our ability to be aware and catch on to trends earlier. The decision to wait or jump in depends entirely on your judgment and is a function of the amount of learning you do about the circumstances around you. In the post-COVID-19 economy, we may see a completely different cycle dynamic. It will certainly be interesting to watch how it unfolds in the years to follow.

Regardless of what happens after our current economic crisis, as long as credit exists and people borrow money, there will be cycles. Ray Dalio, the billionaire founder of the world's most successful hedge fund created an easy to understand video about why this is so. You can find a link to it in the resources section of my website. We owe it to ourselves to understand these cycles and be prepared for opportunity in advance.

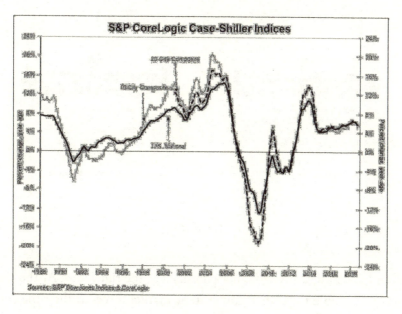

Figure 25

Just like economic cycles, real estate cycles have their opportune chances like stock investing. Of course, in order to seize the opportunities, you have to be ready and have a strategy in place. Markets oscillate up and down, and as an investor, it's our responsibility to pay attention to the national and the local-market activity to identify where we are in the market cycle (Figure 26). We must be aware of what inevitably will come. In our current system, we expect market cycles to take around 7–10 years to go full circle.

Figure 26

Before I even knew my wife, her parents had the right idea. At the time, it was impossible to predict how potent market forces at the time could be. They wanted to help my wife with her graduate school tuition by purchasing a condo for her to live in. In theory, the condo would appreciate, and, after a few years, sell it to pay student loans. Unfortunately, it was purchased exactly one month before the crash in 2008.

Fast forward to 2013 after graduation. It was time for her to start by doing a residency program in a different state, but we had a problem. As we explored some options together about where she could apply and where it might take us, we had to remind ourselves that the property was still underwater, 4–5 years later.

"We owe more on the mortgage than it's worth, so maybe I should look for a position around here," she mumbled. "Unless we could hold onto it and rent it out to some grad students, maybe?" Her voice carried a new sense of hope.

We didn't even think. We ran with it. We started as many others would in our shoes. By googling "how to be a landlord." A few weeks of research, connecting with people, and showing the place, we found some great graduate students that lived there for the entire duration of their school career and were perfect tenants, paying each month on time and never calling for any issues unless it was major.

Figure 27

Then in 2017, when these great tenants had graduated, the market cycle had reached a point again in which the place was worth more than the mortgage and had gained $100,000 in equity. We were able to sell for a modest profit, and that profit went to grow our portfolio even more with cheaper, out-of-state property. This property was a huge lesson for us in market cycles. Because we were willing to wait to catch the next market cycle peak by holding the property through hard times, we made it to the other side and profited from the patience and creativity (Figure 27).

As investors, we should understand the overall picture of the dynamics of change. It will benefit us greatly to be a student of market cycles and try to predict where it will be within a 1–2 year outlook. This will help us plan our investing strategy for the short and long-term in terms of timing to ramp up buying or slow it down.

These terms are important to understand and recognize, but in the end, they are just tools. When I first discovered these concepts, I had already acquired about 5–6 properties. From there, this knowledge helped me determine where, when and why to expand my holdings of a certain type, and compelled me to act quickly rather than be overly cautious. With this knowledge, I understood my buying opportunities would become less lucrative as the market got more competitive if I did not act when I did. This helped me understand I would win in the bigger picture.

Don't think this is the end of learning about market types and cycles, it's only the tip of the iceberg. It's meant to make you aware of what needs to be mastered and "felt," via direct experience of getting your first dollar of equity into the winds of market dynamics and cycle timing. Think of it as more of a benchmark or basic vocabulary term that other investors use to refer to the current investment climate.

RETURNS AND INDICATORS—MEASURES OF SUCCESS

Once we know the basics of real estate markets and have a true understanding of the cycles, the next important item to grasp is returns. Returns are what we live for and are our incentive and reward when we deploy our hard-earned capital into a real estate investment. Knowing the basic terms, and how these are calculated, will go a long way in communicating with other investors. This will help you to benchmark your own investments and make comparisons to the profits you're making versus placing your money to work in other areas.

Let's start with the most basic of formulas for investment property:

NOI (Net Operating Income) = Income - Expenses

The NOI will help you understand how self-sustaining your property is. If your property has more income than expenses (which we should expect to see) the NOI will be positive.

Cash Flow = NOI - Financing Costs = Income - (Expenses + Financing)

Cash flow is the true measure of the property performance. This takes into account your cost of financing the operation of your property. The financing that one investor has available to them may not be the same as others due to varying levels of investor credit, experience, timing, etc. You should shoot for positive numbers, around $100 or more. The more the better. It is up to you to decide exactly what you are willing to accept, but $100 per unit with conservative guesses on expenses has worked well for me.

CAP (Capitalization) Rate = NOI / Purchase Price

The cap rate, introduced earlier in this chapter, helps describe how hard a deployed outlay of cash is working for you to fetch a return. This metric excludes financing (since that varies from investor to investor). The cap rate is therefore an "apples to apples" often used to describe the nature of the property and how it is expected to behave, regardless of the investor operating it. This is the most common metric used as a screening criteria for purchasing individual rental properties, or when communicating with other investors.

C-o-C (Cash-on-Cash Return) = Cash Flow / Cash Outlay To Purchase Only

Cash on cash is the king of metrics in multifamily investing and describes a personalized rate of return on a true dollar-for-dollar basis, taking into consideration any financing or leverage (mortgage or debt service). The higher the leverage on the property, the lower the cash outlay to purchase it. Financing payments may also increase which, in turn, decreases your cash flow. Depending on your situation, C-o-C could vary quite a bit. In multifamily, the managers fix a C-o-C return target for the investors who join in the investment.

ROE (Return on Equity) = (Cash flow + Appreciation + Debt Paydown) / Total Investment Equity

This sophisticated term helps investors understand more accurately how hard their *equity* is working for them (as opposed to cash). In places where appreciation and cash flow effects are visible, keeping track of this metric in a portfolio will help an investor decide when to reallocate equity elsewhere or convert to debt to obtain more assets, depending on the investor's risk appetite.

ROI (Return on Investment) = (Cash flow + Appreciation + Debt Paydown) / Total Investment Value

Similar to the Return on Equity metric, this figure helps get closer to what our true return on the property is at a given time. This is a great way to weigh out opportunity costs versus other investments, such as stocks, bonds, businesses and other investment vehicles.

Take a look at Figure 28 to get an understanding of these formulas and measures of financial performance for a fixed investment property.

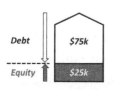

Purchase Price:	$100,000
Rental Income:	$1,050
Expenses (Monthly)	
Property Taxes:	-$100
Insurance:	-$60
Property Management:	-$105
Maintenance:	-$50
CAPEX:	-$50
Vacancy (3 weeks / yr):	-$70
Net Operating Income:	**$615**
Financing (5%, 30 yr):	-$403
Cash Flow (Monthly):	**$212**

Net Operating Income (NOI) = Income – Expenses (Tax, Insurance, etc.)

= $1050 - $100 - $60 - $105 - $50 - $50 - $70
= **$615**

Cash Flow = NOI – Financing Costs (Mortgage, Line of Credit, etc.)

= $615 - $403
= **$212**

Capitalization (Cap) Rate = Annual NOI / Purchase Price

= ($615 x 12) / $100,000
= 0.0738 or **7.4%**

Cash-on-Cash (C-o-C) Return = Cash Flow / Cash Outlay (Down, Rehab, etc.)

= ($212 x 12) / ($25,000 + $0 + $0)
= 0.0102 or **10.2%**

Assuming a 3% appreciation rate and hold for 3 years....

Return on Equity (ROE) = (Total Cash Flow + Appr. + Debt Paydown) / (Total Investment Equity)

= (($212 x 12 x 3) + $9,272 + $3,701) / ($25,000 + $9,272)

= 0.601 or **60.1%**

Figure 28

YOUR PRIVATE RESIDENCE VS. RENTAL PROPERTIES

If you are a working professional privileged enough to own your own home, I would like to make a few distinctions between a homestead versus a rental property. Many of the same physical concepts (such as lot size, maintenance, appliances, roofs, etc.) are the same if you choose to build a rental property portfolio, but there are subtle differences in other aspects of homes treated as rentals as opposed to your personal residence.

FINANCING

Oftentimes, lenders writing loans for investors while purchasing a rental property are going to be more strict on down payments. The difference is that they normally require down payments of 20–25% to meet the loan to value requirements of 80-75%. This is different in a private residence, where you can be in a home for almost no money down if it is your principal residence (anywhere from 0 to 15% is commonplace for owners with middle-class incomes and good credit). In addition, mortgages on rental property have slightly higher interest rates and if you plan to cash-out refinance, you'll get hit with slightly higher interest (although, at the time of this writing in the pre-coronavirus economy in Q1 of 2020, should still be around 5–6%). If you use your personal name on the title of the property, your debt-to-income ratio (DTI) that all lenders use to evaluate your financial health and readiness could be affected if you are planning on buying another private residence. It takes a year or two for your lender to count your rental income coming in to offset any existing mortgages you have on rental properties. It would be prudent to find and consult a good mortgage broker who can assist you with your loans in shopping for the lowest rate and answer any questions you may have.

TO LLC OR NOT TO LLC

If you place properties into an LLC before closing, that LLC is treated as a separate entity apart from you. You own it and the profits flow to you. As a distinction from principal primary residences, you do have the option to place your rental properties into an LLC, but usually not your homestead.

Many investors elect to put their investments in LLC's. There are advantages and drawbacks to doing this, including financing options that are variable and higher insurance premiums. There are lots of conversations held online you can follow to determine if you should hold title in an LLC or not. This particular discussion is out of the scope of this book.

1031 EXCHANGES

Your real estate investment properties can be exchanged so all the equity you gain can be re-leveraged without capital gains. They are instead deferred. Take a look at Figure 29. 1031 Exchanges can be used to exchange properties as long as you maintain who or whatever entity is on title from one property to the next. In this way, it is possible for you to defer paying capital gains taxes *for life*. You'd be able to pass along properties to your heirs at a stepped-up basis when you die, which means those capital gains would be erased forever. Unfortunately, this is not something you can do with your primary residence. Only rental property or real estate viewed as business use qualifies for this exemption.

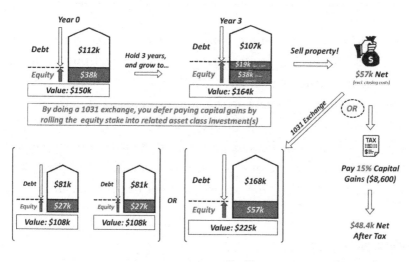

Figure 29

ASSET VS. LIABILITY

In Robert Kiyosaki's book, "Rich Dad, Poor Dad," it explained anything that places money in your pocket is an asset while anything that takes money out is a liability. Your primary residence, however, is a maintenance machine and requires upkeep, utilities, mortgage, and more, all of which take money out of your pocket. A rental investment, on the other hand, is by its nature an investment and must put money in your pocket in order to make sense to own. If you do your numbers right, any plumbing repair, roof issue, carpet replacement, etc. is accounted for in your underwriting and should still flow profit over a holding period. If this happens in your own home, it's on you. While many people view their home as an asset because it increases in value, you only get to realize that gain when you sell it. It costs you money every month to live in it. This means that your private residence is actually a liability while you are living in it. Rentals on the other hand, are designed to be assets.

CREATIVE OPERATION

You can do many fancy things such as offering lease options to your tenants and become their bank. This allows you to exit from the property management, maintenance and taxes equation. Residents become owners and you own the note on the house you've issued to them. If they miss payments, you can take title back in the form of foreclosure. Other things can be done with distressed property that includes mortgage wraps and so forth, but I'm not an expert on these methods and they are also beyond the scope of this book so they will not be discussed here further.

EXPENSE WRITE-OFFS

In rental properties, you have the ability to write off all your expenses related to the rental property. That includes insurance, property taxes, maintenance, property management, and even mortgage or financing interest, if you have any. As mentioned in previous chapters, you can also write off travel expenses if you visit the property for any business-related reason. These expenses come off the bottom line of your profits, reducing your personal taxable income.

RENTAL GRADE

While it may be tempting to add granite countertops in your C-class rental property because that's what *you* would want, *you* are not living there. You should not spend the money because you will not recover those invested dollars easily in rent premiums. It may not be standard or expected for that submarket and property class. Resist the urge to over-glam your rentals and stay in line with the finishes the area demands.

LOCATION & OBJECTIVE

Your rentals will go weeks, months, or even years without you seeing them. This sounds odd, but you have a team (property manager) to do this for you. This is business, not your home to decorate and impress others with. Treat your investments as a partnership with the team and the residents living there. Provide a safe living space with nice touches and expect your residents to pay on time. Professionalism in understanding that "it's just business" is a must. If you are in doubt as to whether or not you need a property manager for a local rental, you probably do. I highly recommend one even if you can do it, because it'll teach you to be business-oriented and keep your thoughts on buying the next property and not maintaining what you have.

You now have a basic grasp on the vocabulary, math and perspective to start thinking about which path of investing in real estate to embark. In the next few chapters, I'll provide my blueprint of how I was able to build my single-family portfolio relatively quickly and what process I used to do this on a part-time basis with a demanding full-time job. In the next chapter, we'll take a closer look at what you have to work with financially in getting started with your own portfolio.

ACTION STEPS

➢ If you're still confused about any of the topics discussed, write them down here. Be sure to look online or reread anything you found to be unclear.

_____

_____

_____

➢ Consider the market cycle where you live now. Think about the local and national cycles occurring right now. Is your market on the upswing with activity heating up and high competition for housing? Or, is it cooling off with prices lowering and buyers having more control? How does this compare to the national economic market cycle? Are they at the same point on the curve in your opinion?

_____

_____

_____

➢ What is the cap-rate average in the area you live in?

➢ Give what you think about market cycles and cap rates, what high level strategy do you have to buy? Will you wait or try to buy as soon as possible? Will you buy in your backyard, or look elsewhere?

_____

_____

_____

CHAPTER 9

TAKING STOCK OF SEEDS

"You don't need to start great but you have to start to be great." —Joe Sabath

WHEN FIRST BUILDING my real estate holdings, I started with some theoretical knowledge from a few months of listening to podcasts and began saving my money. I knew buying houses meant saving for down payments, so this became my approach. I worked hard in the office, building my store of knowledge and shifting my attention into growing cash seed funds. While it's true you can start with little to no money down in real estate, it's not the primary approach I advocate while you are working. It increases your risk and essentially signs you up for another job because margins are usually so thin.

I feel, as an investor and entrepreneur, we need to be true to our "competitive advantage" wherever we can. Since we are also working professionals, our true strength is our steady income. This will help us start with cash and allow us to easily qualify for loans.

FINANCIAL READINESS

I highly recommend you put yourself in a position where you are cash-flow positive each month for your household's finances. By doing this, not only are you starting to save cash, but you are also giving yourself a margin of safety in case something goes wrong. In either case, by getting your household finances away from the paycheck-to-paycheck situation, you're building a stronger financial future for yourself. Take a minute to review your financial situation. Are you in the red each month? If you don't know, look back at your bank statements and see how much, if anything, you've been saving each month. It will become apparent if you've made a large purchase or a series of small purchases. It's time to dial back on these to build a war chest for yourself.

This will put you in a place to invest and win in the long term. Consider the wealth equation below:

$$Wealth = (offense + defense + knowledge) * consistency$$

In this case, offense is your income and investments while defense is the money you save. Knowledge allows you to pull levers and seek high returns with disproportionately low risk, and consistency is the action taking mindset that sticks with you over time. Are you living this equation? If so, you're on track and are most likely financially ready to move forward already. If not, it doesn't take long to get there. Read on to find out about more resources to help you on your financial journey.

YOU MAY HAVE MORE THAN YOU THINK

There are plenty of places that you, as a savvy investor, can source funds for your first investment. Using each of these areas has pros and cons that may apply to your situation. Only you know what is most appropriate for you.

- *Cash*: The most straightforward and liquid form of value. There may not be much, but if there is, you are in good shape. If not, you can start building this on the side.
- *Home Equity*: Your private residence is a store of value. You can tap into this using a home equity line of credit (HELOC) at low rates, which allows you to fully purchase properties that return money at a higher rate than you are borrowing. This is one way to build massive wealth quickly.
- *Personal Lines*: If you have fantastic credit and a good income, some banks or lending institutions will advance personal lines (credit unions are well known for this) just for "being you."
- *IRA's*: If you have an old 401(k) or 403(b) from a previous employer, you can convert it to what is called an SD-IRA (self-directed individual retirement account) or a QRP (qualified retirement plan) and treat those funds as cash. The only catch: this money behaves like a 401(k) in which you can't take any cash out of the account penalty-free until you qualify and you are 59.5 years old. Your income from the property you buy within your SD-IRA accounts keeps building up, like a bank account. You cannot convert 401(k) funds with your current employer, but if you've rolled previous 401(k) funds into your current 401(k), you may be able to move those out into a new SD-IRA.
- *Other Assets:* There may be items to sell in your house. Perhaps you have some artwork or china that can fetch some cash. Or, maybe you have some stock or other assets like jewelry savings bonds, maturing certificates of deposits (CD's) or artwork.

You may have more than you think—right now. Thinking of alternative ways to start investing will lower the bar and make it easier for you to get serious in investing in your first property.

RESOURCE READINESS

These resources have served me well as I moved forward investing part-time while working full time. Please take advantage of these resources below. Many changed my perspective when I needed it. They will also have a profound impact on your investing and personal lives.

http://elevateequity.org/the-book/book-resources/

Keep in mind that none of these resources are a substitute for action. These should be used mainly during your process of taking action when questions arise.

I hope you're feeling more ready and prepared at this point. There's been a lot to digest in previous chapters. Ideally you've found there's more than you thought in the financial and resource readiness areas. Now, we're ready to use them in the single-family realm in the next chapter.

ACTION STEPS

➢ Go to the Resources webpage and download a copy of the net worth calculator. To the best of your ability (and without getting into too many of the details) list all of your assets and liabilities. Fill out the form completely, tallying up all of your income sources and expenses. Is there room for investing in real estate? Where will it come from? Your stored capital or your monthly income?

➢ Pick any 3 books from the links at the resources site listed above and purchase these books or audio books. We want to build up your backlog of empowering and/or useful information to increase your curiosity and keep you motivated.

Book #1: _____

Book #2: _____

Book #3: _____

CHAPTER 10

MY BLUEPRINT FOR SINGLE-FAMILY SUCCESS

"Real estate cannot be lost or stolen, nor can it be carried away, purchased with common sense, paid in full, and managed with reasonable care, it is about the safest investment in the world." —Franklin D. Roosevelt

IN THE FOLLOWING pages, we'll jump into how I was able to build a portfolio of properties within a year. If you do live in a market where it may make sense to invest directly with buy and hold (medium to high cap rates), you have a distinct advantage for success. If not, you can still make it work by investing at a distance as I have done. I'm providing my perspective and giving you the nuts and bolts of how to do this in the coming pages. In the book "Long Distance Real Estate Investing," the author, David Greene, walks you through the direct tactics he uses. I highly recommend serious investors read it when starting out. You can find his book in the Resources section of our website.

By following the path provided in this chapter, you may be able to retire either your partner or yourself from your full-time job.

Take my mother-in-law, for example. By acquiring single family homes that were already cash flowing at purchase, she was able to retire from her physically demanding job. In addition to the repetitive physical demands at work, her boss was borderline combative and created a toxic work environment. Working increased her blood pressure, decreased her mood, and caused other hormone imbalances from the stress. As soon as her rental properties started to make more than she did at her job, she began to question why she was still working. They have not turned back since then, living life on her own terms. This happened within about 2 to 3 years when they started to treat real estate investing more seriously. This can and will happen for you, too, if you choose and resolve to put your knowledge to work.

WHY SINGLE FAMILY?

Many investors start in single-family homes before trying larger projects. If you have a personality that enjoys getting into the nuts and bolts of how investments work and like to tweak variables, single-family is most likely the best way to start. Some of the amazing benefits of single-family investing include:

- *Control.* You outright own a property with no partners or voting rights to contend with. You have full control of your property.
- *Lower barrier to entry.* While this can also be a disadvantage because of competition for inventory, the concept behind buying a single house seems less intimidating—and it is.
- *Relatively small seed funds.* Starting with a single-family house can be inexpensive if you look in the right places. Compared to most multifamily investments, a single-family home is "reachable" and doesn't require much creativity to understand how to manage it.

- *Variety and choices.* Since your "farm" to choose investment property from include both homeowners and investors like you, options are always out there and always changing.
- *Test your team.* Seeing how well your team (of contacts) works on a small scale with one property will give you an indication of how it will work with multiple properties. If they don't perform to your expectations, you can change them out for someone else relatively easy.
- *Lower vacancies.* If you have a happy family in your rental property and the rates are fair, you can potentially have the same resident stay for years. This isn't likely in places like apartments where turnover is much greater. It's highly unusual to find a resident who will stay in the same apartment unit for decades, let alone years.

START WITH YOUR CRITERIA

Before finding property, we will need to narrow your focus. There are plenty of houses available at any one time, so take a moment to think about your ideal property. Obviously, it would be amazing to have one provide 40% cash-on-cash return each year, with no headaches, and double in value over three years. This is simply too high a bar for your first property. Remember: your goal should be to *learn* with this first property and *take action*. That will curb any Analysis Paralysis tendencies. Examples of major criteria I've used in the past to help narrow my focus is:

- *Cap Rate.* This is huge and helps eliminate areas within your market. What you decide here will determine if you are a cash-flow investor, an appreciation investor (which I don't recommend), or a hybrid with components of both. If you aim for a Cap Rate of 8%, most likely, you'll find yourself in the midwest. Take a look at the commercial real estate cap rate survey performed by CBRE in Figure 30 from the first half of

2019. Targeting cap rates encapsulates your investing goals with a starting point to eliminate markets or submarkets that don't make sense.

- *Type of Property.* Are you looking for a condo, single-family house, duplex, triplex, or fourplex? Generally, it's best to start with a single-family house with no HOA's. Small multifamily properties may seem more attractive at first because of the higher income for the cash outlay. However, these have more potential for issues with utilities, transient tenants, and resale value because it is assumed that your end buyer will be another investor rather than a local homeowner. Smaller multifamily properties also tend to be located in older areas with higher density, so your chances of appreciation may not be as good as single families. This is general advice that can have some exceptions in certain markets, but I've found this to be true most of the time.

- *Price.* Whatever amount you are willing to invest out-of-pocket, take half and use as your down payment and 3 months of operation. Knowing this number for target pricing will help you immensely later on. Whatever you don't use can be allocated for the next property or used for an emergency in your personal situation.

- *The "1% Rule."* This is a simple rule of thumb to determine whether a property will have net positive cash flow. If you find monthly rents for properties you are looking at are at least 1% of the purchase price, then there's a strong likelihood of being net positive on cash flow. For example, if a $100,000 rental property rents for $1,100, is the 1% rule satisfied? To check this, we ask: is $1,100 greater than 1% of $100,000? Since $100,000 x 1% = $1,000 and $1,100 in rental income is higher than 1%, or $1,000 per month, it passes this test.

U.S. MULTIFAMILY INFILL | FIGURE 51: KEY RATES CONT.

	CLASS A				CLASS B				CLASS C			
	CAP RATES FOR STABILIZED PROPERTIES (%)	CHANGE	EXPECTED RETURN ON COST FOR VALUE-ADD PROPERTIES (%)	CHANGE	CAP RATES FOR STABILIZED PROPERTIES (%)	CHANGE	EXPECTED RETURN ON COST FOR VALUE-ADD PROPERTIES (%)	CHANGE	CAP RATES FOR STABILIZED PROPERTIES (%)	CHANGE	EXPECTED RETURN ON COST FOR VALUE-ADD PROPERTIES (%)	CHANGE
TIER I												
Atlanta	4.25-5.00	⇔	5.50-6.25	⇔	5.00-5.75	⇔	6.25-6.75	⇔	5.75-6.50	⇔	6.50-7.25	⇔
Austin	4.00-4.50	▼	4.00-4.50	▼	4.25-4.75	▼	4.25-4.75	▼	4.50-5.25	⇔	4.50-5.25	▼
Baltimore	4.50-5.00	⇔	5.25-5.75	⇔	5.00-5.75	⇔	6.00-6.75	⇔	6.00-6.75	⇔	7.00-8.00	⇔
Charlotte	4.50-5.00	⇔	4.75-5.25	⇔	5.00-5.50	⇔	4.75-5.25	⇔	5.75-6.25	⇔	5.50-6.00	⇔
Dallas/Ft. Worth	4.50-5.00	⇔	5.00-5.50	⇔	5.00-6.00	⇔	6.00-7.00	⇔	5.75-6.25	⇔	6.75-7.25	⇔
Denver	4.25-5.00	⇔	5.75-6.25	▼	5.00-5.50	⇔	6.00-7.00	▼	5.25-5.75	⇔	6.75-7.25	▼
Houston	4.00-4.50	▼	4.75-5.25	▼	4.75-5.25	▼	5.25-5.75	▼	5.50-6.00	▼	6.25-6.75	▼
Minneapolis/St. Paul	4.50-5.00	⇔	5.00-5.50	⇔	5.00-5.25	⇔	5.50-6.00	⇔	5.00-5.50	⇔	5.75-6.25	⇔
Nashville	4.50-5.00	⇔	4.25-5.75	⇔	5.00-5.50	⇔	5.25-5.75	⇔	5.50-6.00	▼	6.00-6.50	⇔
Orlando	4.50-5.00	⇔	—		4.50-5.00	▼	5.25-5.75	▼	5.25-5.75	▼	6.00-6.50	▼
Philadelphia	4.50-5.00	▼	5.75-6.75	▼	5.50-6.00	⇔	6.75-7.75	⇔	6.00-6.75	⇔	7.00-7.75	⇔
Phoenix	4.25-5.00	▼	5.50-6.00	⇔	4.25-5.00	▼	5.50-6.25	▼	4.75-5.25	▼	5.75-6.50	▼
Portland	4.50-4.75	⇔	4.75-5.00	⇔	4.75-5.00	⇔	5.00-5.25	⇔	5.00-5.25	▲	5.25-5.50	⇔
Raleigh-Durham	4.25-5.00	⇔	5.25-5.75	⇔	5.00-5.75	⇔	6.00-6.50	⇔	5.50-6.00	⇔	6.00-6.50	⇔
Sacramento	4.75-5.25	▲	5.25-6.00	⇔	5.00-5.50	▲	5.50-6.50	⇔	5.25-5.75	⇔	5.50-6.50	⇔
Tampa	4.50-5.00	⇔	5.00-5.50	⇔	4.75-5.25	⇔	5.50-6.00	⇔	5.50-6.00	⇔	6.25-7.25	⇔

	CLASS A				CLASS B				CLASS C			
	CAP RATES FOR STABILIZED PROPERTIES (%)	CHANGE	EXPECTED RETURN ON COST FOR VALUE-ADD PROPERTIES (%)	CHANGE	CAP RATES FOR STABILIZED PROPERTIES (%)	CHANGE	EXPECTED RETURN ON COST FOR VALUE-ADD PROPERTIES (%)	CHANGE	CAP RATES FOR STABILIZED PROPERTIES (%)	CHANGE	EXPECTED RETURN ON COST FOR VALUE-ADD PROPERTIES (%)	CHANGE
TIER II												
Albuquerque	5.25-5.50	⇔	6.00-6.50	⇔	5.50-6.00	⇔	6.50-7.00	⇔	6.75-7.25	⇔	7.75-8.75	⇔
Cincinnati	5.00-5.75	⇔	5.75-7.50	⇔	5.25-6.00	⇔	6.50-7.75	⇔	6.00-7.50	▼	7.00-8.50	⇔
Cleveland	5.50-6.25	⇔	7.00-8.00	⇔	6.00-7.00	⇔	8.50-8.75	⇔	8.00-9.00	⇔	9.00-11.00	⇔
Columbus	5.25-5.75	⇔	5.75-6.25	▼	5.50-5.75	▼	6.25-7.50	▼	6.75-8.75	⇔	7.75-8.25	▼
Detroit	6.00-7.00	⇔	6.75-7.50	▼	6.50-7.50	⇔	7.50-8.25	▼	9.00-10.50	⇔	9.50-11.00	⇔
Honolulu	4.75-5.75	⇔	—		3.00-6.00	⇔	—		4.50-6.00	⇔	—	
Indianapolis	5.25-5.50	⇔	6.50-6.75	⇔	5.50-5.75	▼	6.50-6.75	⇔	6.00-6.50	▼	7.25-10.00	⇔
Jacksonville	4.75-5.25	⇔	5.50-6.25	⇔	5.25-6.25	⇔	6.00-7.00	⇔	6.00-6.50	⇔	7.00-7.50	⇔
Kansas City	4.75-5.25	⇔	5.25-5.75	⇔	5.25-5.75	⇔	5.75-6.25	⇔	5.75-6.25	⇔	6.50-7.00	⇔
Memphis	5.25-5.75	⇔	5.50-6.90	⇔	6.00-6.50	⇔	6.25-6.75	⇔	6.75-7.25	⇔	7.00-7.50	⇔
Milwaukee	5.00-5.75	⇔	5.50-6.25	⇔	5.75-6.50	⇔	6.25-7.00	⇔	7.00-8.00	⇔	7.50-8.50	⇔
Oklahoma City	5.25-5.50	▼	6.75-7.00	▼	6.00-6.75	⇔	7.50-8.25	▼	6.75-7.50	▼	8.75-9.50	⇔
Pittsburgh	5.50-6.50	⇔	6.50-7.00	⇔	6.50-7.00	⇔	7.00-7.50	⇔	7.50-8.00	⇔	8.50-9.00	⇔
Salt Lake City	4.50-5.00	⇔	5.25-5.50	⇔	5.00-5.50	⇔	6.00-6.25	▲	5.75-6.25	⇔	6.50-7.00	⇔
San Antonio	4.50-5.25	⇔	4.50-5.25	⇔	4.75-5.50	⇔	4.50-5.25	▼	5.00-5.50	⇔	5.00-5.50	⇔
St. Louis	5.50-5.75	⇔	—		6.00-6.75	⇔	—		7.50-8.50	⇔	—	

CBRE Research

▲ INCREASE
▼ DECREASE
⇔ STABLE
N/A

*Compared with H2 2018. Changes less than 15 bps considered stable.
Source: CBRE Research, Q2 2019.
Notes: Data is subject to historical revision. Markets represented by metropolitan areas. Per larger metros, tier designation is based on the U.S. Census Bureau's combined statistical area (CSA) definitions. Note that MSAs retain same tier designation as the CSA to which they belong.

© 2019 CBRE, Inc. | 50

Figure 30

As I started to look for property, my mentors and research helped attract me to the cash flow and medium to high cap rate markets and properties. I had saved about $30,000, so my target property was around $60,000–$80,000 in price. I was hoping for a cap rate around 8–10%, so my market was in the Midwest. At the time, I didn't know where, but knew this was where my criteria would be met. If you recall in Chapter 1 from my story, this cash got me significantly more property than I thought.

MARKET SELECTION

This is where many investors get stuck. Everyone has a strong opinion about their own market, so when I first started out, this conflicting advice led to confusion and wasn't helpful. When selecting a market include the following considerations.

JOBS AND ECONOMIC OUTLOOK

People cannot move into an area without jobs to support their lifestyle. If job and employment data look strong and the economy is well-diversified, this is a good sign. What we are looking for is data relative to other markets. We want to see job data increasing at levels faster than the US average and with a healthy diversity of industries. To find a good market to invest in, growth is paramount. In order to be able to pay for housing, renters moving in need jobs. We, as investors, need to look for a healthy variety of jobs. Some other criteria to explore are population growth, new construction, and finally income growth in the next 3–7 years. You can find some resources on this on my website, but a great starting point is Google and the Bureau of Labor Statistics, which can offer job data in any market across the country (Figure 31).[12] For example, have any major employers moved in? Are jobs being added faster or slower than the national average here?

Colorado Springs, CO Economy at a Glance:

Data Series	Back Data	July 2019	Aug 2019	Sept 2019	Oct 2019	Nov 2019	Dec 2019
Labor Force Data							
Civilian Labor Force(1)		360.7	360.1	361.5	361.9	362.6	(P) 360.8
Employment(1)		348.4	348.6	352.1	351.8	352.0	(P) 350.8
Unemployment(1)		12.3	11.5	9.4	10.1	10.6	(P) 10.0
Unemployment Rate(2)		3.4	3.2	2.6	2.8	2.9	(P) 2.8
Nonfarm Wage and Salary Employment							
Total Nonfarm(3)		302.0	302.7	303.5	305.4	306.2	(P) 306.0
12-month % change		3.1	2.9	3.3	2.8	3.0	(P) 3.1
Mining, Logging, and Construction(3)		19.6	19.6	19.3	19.4	19.1	(P) 18.8
12-month % change		4.8	5.9	6.0	6.0	4.9	(P) 3.3
Manufacturing(3)		12.1	12.1	12.0	12.1	12.1	(P) 12.1
12-month % change		1.7	1.7	0.8	1.7	2.5	(P) 2.6
Trade, Transportation, and Utilities(3)		45.2	45.5	45.4	46.2	47.8	(P) 47.7
12-month % change		2.5	2.7	2.7	3.6	3.7	(P) 3.7
Information(3)		5.6	5.6	5.6	5.6	5.6	(P) 5.6
12-month % change		-3.4	-1.8	0.0	0.0	-1.8	(P) -1.8
Financial Activities(3)		19.2	19.0	19.0	19.2	19.2	(P) 19.0
12-month % change		2.1	2.2	3.3	2.7	3.8	(P) 2.7
Professional and Business Services(3)		49.3	48.4	47.9	48.0	48.7	(P) 48.8
12-month % change		6.3	4.8	4.1	2.1	3.6	(P) 4.7
Education and Health Services(3)		40.9	41.0	42.0	43.0	42.9	(P) 42.8
12-month % change		5.1	4.6	6.9	5.7	5.7	(P) 4.1
Leisure and Hospitality(3)		40.4	41.3	39.9	38.2	37.4	(P) 37.6
12-month % change		-1.2	0.5	1.3	-2.3	-1.1	(P) 1.3
Other Services(3)		18.2	18.1	17.9	17.9	17.8	(P) 17.8
12-month % change		1.7	1.1	1.7	1.7	1.7	(P) 1.7
Government(3)		51.5	52.1	54.5	55.8	55.6	(P) 55.8
12-month % change		4.3	2.4	2.3	4.1	3.0	(P) 3.0

Figure 31

---

12   https://www.bls.gov/eag/

MARKET CYCLES

Where is the market in relation to others across the country? Is it overbuilt and saturated with renters already? When do you plan on investing and are you going to hold through an entire cycle or buy at the bottom and wait for a rise? How sensitive is this market's economy to that of the nation or world's? It helps to remember local economies have their own market cycles superimposed over the national and global cycles.

GOVERNMENT AND TENANT LAWS

If one town is business-friendly and attracts jobs due to tax incentives, this is a great market to look at. Leadership and organization at the top make it easier for people to get ahead and hire more people. Another aspect to consider is tenant and landlord laws, which give you an idea of how much support courts will give if you ever have to go the legal route for an eviction or dispute. Some states require longer notice times from landlords for various actions, such as rent increases, or lease termination, among other requirements as demonstrated in Figure 32.[13]

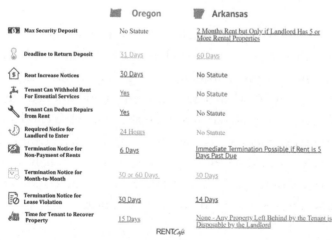

Figure 32

---

13 https://www.rentcafe.com/blog/renting/states-best-worst-laws-renters/

PERSONAL CONNECTIONS

If you have family in a market, that can be huge because you'll be able to write off trips to visit your property. If familiar with a town, you'll have an intuitive grasp where you'd like to invest. Although you typically don't need it, you can also ask your friends or family to help you out if you have an issue that would best be resolved if someone was physically present. This is very powerful for acquiring new properties and checking on existing operations. In these areas, you'll have a distinctive edge over "foreign" investors.

AMENITIES AND SEASONALITY

Be aware of major economic drivers such as dependence on snowfall in mountain and ski areas. In other parts of the country, import / export activity can be affected by trade and manufacturing is dependent on tariff activity. Government job centers, such as military bases, can be good, but also deadly if they decide to close doors. You can really dive into the weeds here, but what is needed is a simple understanding of expectations.

Substantial research into one or a few of these market angles can give you a leg up on other investors and help build your confidence. For instance, while building up my portfolio of single-family homes, I selected Indianapolis in 2016 when I saw upward momentum in the market cycle. Other aspects of market screening also seemed to check out, and I bought properties there to take advantage of the cycle. Doubling down on this strategy turned out to be great, because as I bought up housing there, I saw not only great income, but modest appreciation and stable debt paydown forces adding to my total net worth.

After taking all of the above into account and comparing different markets that meet your criteria, it's time for you to select one and get started. Don't get too scientific here. You can always change your market later, so just choose one that's best now for the sake of taking action. If anything, being flexible in this way will help you develop skills to find newer emerging markets.

Now that we have screened our market, this is where we look at what is available there. We'll dive into which properties to select for purchase and how we expect that property to perform.

UNDERWRITING RENTAL PROPERTY

When I started doing this, I was confident I'd find something and overly optimistic everything would be sunshine and roses. Of course, it didn't turn out that way, but at least I was able to protect my downside by conservative underwriting practices.

Underwriting may seem complicated but is generally straightforward after you get the hang of it. It is composed of two major pieces. One is cash flow, done methodically like a science, and the other is value, which is more like an art form. Let's explore both of these approaches carefully and individually.

CASH-FLOW UNDERWRITING

In order to understand how to underwrite a property for its cash flow, we need to go over possible expenses you could face. We'll then start to put assumptions together that will build an "expected" performance on the property over an extended period. This fully describes the operational aspects of this first LEGO block of an investment. Here common expenses that you should underwrite for single-family properties:

- *Property Management.* The fee your manager takes for being the boots-on-the-ground point of contact. Often this is 10%–8% of collected rent in cash-flow markets, but can be as low as 5%–6% in appreciation markets. Be aware of leasing, tenant placement and call-out fees (when PM's have to visit the site or send someone out) for maintenance.
- *Property Taxes.* Can be looked up on county websites or estimated easily from Zillow or Redfin data.
- Insurance. Also can be looked up. Usually around $500–$800 per house per year, but can be different. Zillow or Redfin is a good starting point.
- *Maintenance & Repairs.* A good rule of thumb is to use 5% of rent for houses in good order and up to 10% or even 15% of rental income for houses in disrepair. We don't recommend taking over a property in a poor condition without doing rehabs up front. This would invite the need for high maintenance reserves. When operating your property, this expense is usually the biggest wildcard.
- *CAPEX.* An expense set aside for major repairs, such as a roof, water heater, furnace or AC unit. We usually set aside 5%–10% of rents, depending on the condition of property and its age.
- *Vacancy.* The vacancy average across the country is currently three weeks. If there's no one in your property, you aren't getting paid. This should be accounted in our numbers proactively.

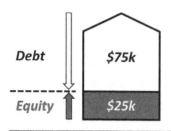
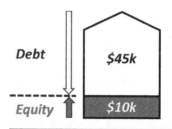

123 Wellwritten Ave		999 Confusion St.	
Purchase Price:	$100,000	Purchase Price:	$55,000
Rental Income:	$1,050	Rental Income:	$1,100
Expenses		Expenses	
Property Taxes:	-$100	Property Taxes:	-$200
Insurance:	-$60	Insurance:	-$30
Property Management:	-$105	Property Management:	-$40
Maintenance:	-$50	Maintenance:	$0
CAPEX:	-$50	CAPEX:	$0
Vacancy (3 weeks / yr):	-$70	Vacancy (3 weeks / yr):	-$50
Net Operating Income:	$615	Net Operating Income:	$780
Financing (5%, 30 yr):	-$403	Financing (5%, 30 yr):	-$242
Cash Flow:	$212	Cash Flow:	$538
Cap. Rate:	7.4%	Cap. Rate:	17.0%

Figure 33

Take a look at Figure 33 to see an example of two properties being underwritten to evaluate whether or not to purchase. One is underwritten well (conservative and achievable), and the other is not (overly aggressive, unrealistic and misguided). It should be easy to identify which is which.

As for the rents you'll receive, there are many places where you can get data, including Zillow Rentals, Redfin, Craigslist and Rent-o-meter (which is not free, but highly recommended). You can piece together information and get a feel for what a prospective tenant might pay based on this property's competition, adjusting rent slightly for some different square footage, numbers of bedrooms/baths, and pictures of appliances and finishes in the property. Use your renter hat and pretend what you'd be willing to pay, given the other options nearby. Once you're outside of the neighborhood and out of "comps," naturally, the data gets less accurate. Eventually, you'll get a feel for what kind of rents you'll be able to command. Your property manager should also be able to give you their thoughts before you even get into contract.

VALUE UNDERWRITING

To underwrite and check the value of the property, we'll have to go into some terms, especially if you are looking to rehab or do work on a property to get it rent ready. Terms to know:

- *Purchase Price*. Price at which the property is for sale.
- *Rehab*. Estimated cost of the construction to get it ready to rent (or to flip).
- *ARV (After Repair Value)*. Value at which we think the property will be after repairs.

A successful rehab project will see the purchase price and rehab cost in a property lower than the finished house value. Let's look at an example to see how this works. In Figure 34, a house is identified in a neighborhood that only costs about $80,000 when everything around it is going for $150,000. In most cases, it's because the house has big problems and needs major repairs. If you can get your purchase price and rehab investment for less than what the property would sell after repairs, you'd have bonus equity which we can call your "profit." Later, we will see clever options to make best use of this profit that doesn't involve selling, but rather keeping it for yourself.

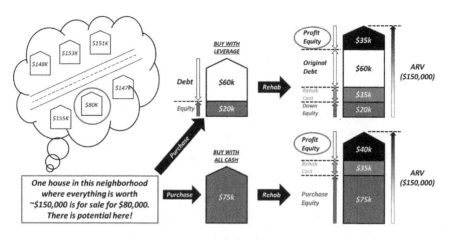

Figure 34

Now it's time to pause so you can try this out yourself. Please refer to the action points at the end of this chapter and immediately dedicate a time block in your calendar to do them. Only you can create your future, so it's time to take concrete steps to manifest it.

If you require more help and need an example of how to do this, I've created a video to walk you through a property yourself. This video is located here:

http://elevateequity.org/the-book/getting-started-with-underwriting/

I recommend it's done in a spreadsheet either you create or find online. Obviously, creating your own is best due to the learning opportunity it presents and allows you to take advantage of the repeatable and scalable skill tool we mentioned earlier. I also have an underwriting template available in the Premium Resources Section of my website in case you get stuck. Information on how to access that section can be found later in the book (keep on reading!).

Underwriting is a major skill that will help you call out B.S. for anything presented to you, including a poor PM. Once you understand how this works, you'll see how easy it is for someone to present a 20% cap rate property to someone who doesn't know any better.

By now, you should have selected a market to study. Don't worry if you are not positive about your choice now; the important thing to do is to pick one and do some underwriting to add to your toolbelt of abilities. You should also have underwritten some properties and gotten a feel for what rents look like in the area.

We have now come to an important decision to make. Will you do this on your own, or should you pay someone to do all the work for you?

TO TURNKEY OR NOT TO TURNKEY...

Up to now, we've gotten a little glimpse of the microcosms that comprise decisions in buying a property. Now, we really have to ask ourselves what type of investor we want to be starting in the single-family / small multifamily (less than four units) route.

There are providers that offer fully rehabbed properties with a tenant and property management already in place. From the very day of closing, you are collecting rent. While this seems pretty amazing at first glance you should be cautious. This is exactly why we encourage investors to understand how to underwrite properties themselves, educating themselves so they won't be swindled.

Note: when selecting an investment, there will be both operator (who is offering the turnkey property) and property considerations (the property itself). Here's some key things to consider when evaluating turnkey providers you may find online.

- *Reputation.* What do people say about the turnkey provider in the open forums at Bigger Pockets and through Google and

Yelp? Does anyone in your network of real estate contacts / acquaintances know this company or know anyone who has invested with them?
- *Appearance & Professionalism.* If you call to talk with them or look at their holdings online, what does your gut tell you? Are they overpriced? Too heavy on marketing? Not organized? Do you think they are missing pictures of certain rooms / areas of the property?
- *Property Management.* This is probably the largest success or failure factor (measured by happiness or frustration) for investors that largely determines how long investors stick with real estate investing. Your PM will be partnered with you for the medium term. You must screen and call these folks with many questions. Are you able to select your own PM before closing or are you stuck with them for a while? For a more extensive list of questions to pick form, refer to the Resources Section of our website from Chapter 9.
- *All-in-one-ness.* Did the PM or turnkey provider do the rehab directly? Are they willing to ensure the construction quality if something breaks or malfunctions by providing a warranty to the construction?
- *Connections.* If you are referred to a turnkey provider by someone happy with the company, you have the power of that person as leverage with the provider. Meaning that if you are not happy with their product, you can express that through your connection to attract more attention from the turnkey provider or PM if needed.
- *Heart of Teachers.* If the turnkey provider seems untrustworthy and tries to deceive you before you hang up the phone, this is not a good sign. Listen to your gut.

Then, when it comes to evaluating the actual property, there will be additional items to consider:

- *Underwriting.* Underwrite the property, estimating what the fair value is *yourself*, and evaluate the target rents. Take into consideration size, beds, baths, year built, layout, amenities and features and finishes based on what you see within a 0.25-mile radius of the house. Compare your underwriting with theirs. In some cases you may not see expenses like maintenance or vacancy in a turnkey providers' return calculations. Watch out for this because it could be a red flag.
- *Location.* Is this in a war zone? Will it be the only nice house in a block of run-down homes? Who will want to live here? Is it in the "path of progress" and does it have good medium to long-term growth prospects? Does it look like positive change is headed this way?
- *Nearby Houses.* Are there many active rehabs happening in the area? This means it is transitioning and would be a great spot to buy and wait. If all the homes in the area are newer or stable, you're in an area that is mature and can expect stable rents.
- *Photos.* Be sure you have enough photos of all the rooms in the house and possibly even a video. If you don't have this, you are flying blind and will not be able to make an informed decision.
- *Terms.* If you are buying all-cash, be cautious if there is pressure for quick closes such as 15 days or less. Always make sure you have an inspection done. No exceptions. You can look up inspectors on Google or Yelp or Bigger Pockets. Make sure you can back out of the contract if you find something serious that you were not expecting.
- *Lenders Allowed.* If the provider requires you to close all in cash, this means a lender, who will be running a comps analysis to determine the loan amount allowed for the property, may not place the same value on the property as your turnkey provider. That's a clear warning light. Often, higher risk and higher return properties that are cheap run into this issue. If a lender welcomes loans on the property, that means a bank is willing to stand beside you and support your purchase. This is what you want.

In Figure 35 you'll find an example of what a turnkey operator will offer in some of their investment cut sheets. I've marked up a few thoughts to consider, based on preliminary due diligence for this particular investment. These thoughts would help me have a conversation and provide a guide for my negotiations with the seller when talking about purchasing it.

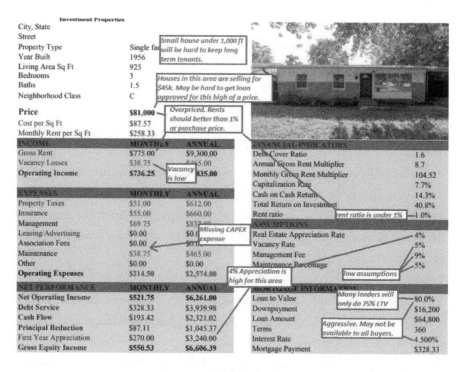

Figure 35

DECISION POINT ON TURNKEYS

Now, there's another big decision to make. Do you decide to go with a turnkey? Or do you do it yourself, meaning you're on your own to select your agent, PM, contractor and lender?

The answer depends on you and your personality. If you enjoy talking to people and getting your hands dirty or are willing to spend a little more time getting started to save a few dollars, then it may make sense to do it. However, if you are short on time, have dollars to invest and want to see how it works first before you go further, turnkey may be right for you.

I must point out selecting a turnkey provider for the first few investments in a market is fine. This is what I did to build confidence and teach myself the basics. Debates on whether or not you should start out with turnkey rentals are all over the internet, but I think these websites get it all wrong. You should do whatever will get you to *take action* the quickest.

Eventually and organically, you'll become more and more of a student in your market and find properties through an agent, getting recommendations from there. The most successful investors are engaged with their investments. While they may seem passive and can act that way, it is much better when you are actively involved with the managers and keep tabs on your investments, much like what you would do with a stock portfolio.

If going turnkey is not something you want to do, congratulations. This is the more dedicated, slow to start, but higher knowledge and higher return model. Taking this route is quite a process, which I would be happy to outline for you here. My good friend, David Greene, co-host of the Bigger Pockets podcast, has written several books on this process. I have adapted several of my techniques from him in buying properties out of state. Check out his books in the resources section in Chapter 9 for his approach. My personal path took much longer than necessary due to barriers I imposed on myself discussed in previous chapters. To see how I did that to myself, check out the Gannt chart in Figure 36 for the high-level view of how I went step-by-step through to my first non-turnkey property.

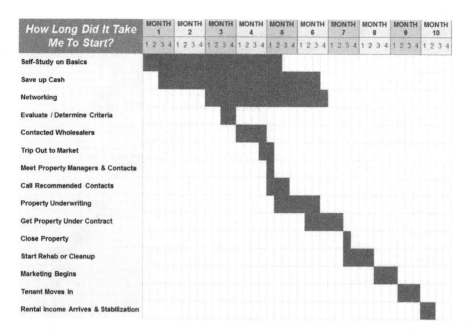

Figure 36

Looking back, it seems like I took a long time from deciding to invest to receiving my first rental income payment. Luckily, going through the process at least one time gives you confidence and clarity that drives quicker action. The second property went faster and more efficiently as my contacts were established and I needed less guidance (Figure 37). The subsequent properties were even faster as I received emails with pre-screened properties that met my criteria.

Your personal timeline may vary dramatically from mine due to your risk temperament, physical location and proximity to your market, time dedicated each day, financial resources, etc.

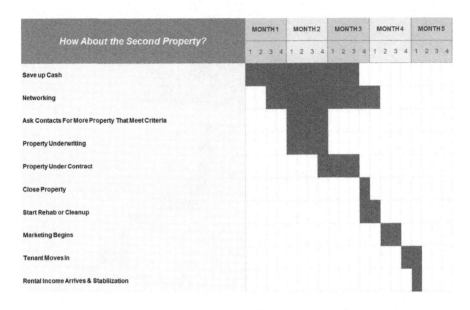

Figure 37

In countless online resources on the same topic, the term "building a team" seemed so intimidating to me, especially when starting out. Because of that, I've gone out of my way to avoid using this term.

David Greene, in his book, "Long Distance Real Estate Investing" refers to the Core 4: Agents, Property Managers, Contractors, and Lenders. When I started out, I simply interviewed agents and property managers since these folks are the most connected in your markets. If your market is out of state, look on Bigger Pockets, Facebook, Yelp, Google, or your personal connections anywhere you can find them. When you do your first in-person visit to the market, line up back-to-back interviews with as many of these people as possible and see who resonates with you. Check facts from one person to another, focusing on learning great areas to invest in your market with your specific criteria. That should always be your main focus when you are speaking with these individuals. By the time you leave that market, you should have a near-complete understanding of what's possible.

PORTFOLIO BUILDING WITH SINGLE FAMILY HOMES

There are different ways to build a great single-family portfolio as a cornerstone of your LEGO empire. Let's take everything you've read and encapsulate it into building your specific business growth plan. These different approaches each have advantages and disadvantages.

STANDARD STACKING

This method involves purchasing new homes over a specified length of time with a down payment. A good goal would be one or two houses per year. Simply save up a down payment, and buy a rental periodically. Over time, you'll have a nice, healthy portfolio to supplement your income. This is the slowest and steadiest method, but requires the least amount of risk or cash up front.

HELOC STACKING

Use a home line of credit to buy a house outright, then use the rental income from that home to pay back your HELOC along with your income. This is similar to Stacking, but using your own house as a bank as opposed to an actual bank. It's much more efficient by avoiding high closing costs for mortgage origination fees. When looking at buying property, the seller considers this as cash, and cash is king. In regards to finding good property, it helps to offer up cash as opposed to financing in Standard Stacking.

POWER HOUSEHACKING

A term that goes beyond that coined by Brandon Turner of BiggerPockets "Househacking" for renting out rooms in your private residence. We haven't reviewed this one yet, but it's pretty clever. You can buy anything up to a 4-plex just like a private residence with very low financing (5% down for conventional loans or even lower for VA / FHA loans). If you move into a 4-plex you'd have to live in one of the four units. In two years, you'll be eligible to get a new private residence loan. You then purchase and move into a new duplex, triplex, or 4-plex while keeping the old one (and replacing the unit you lived in with a renter). See Figure 38 below for a visual on how this would work. You'll have to underwrite pretty well to make sure you're not taking on more risk than you are comfortable with. In addition, you'll be living in a multifamily rather than having your own yard and space. This method can work well if you are comfortable with that.

When my wife and I moved to California, we had already purchased our first rental and had been out of cash. After a while, we had built up a small nest egg and started to drive around some of the "blue-collar" parts of town, driving by many condos, duplexes and triplexes trying to find something that would fit in our budget. When we drove by a house that had an in-law unit and was located in a nice area, we knew we wanted it right away.

Our idea was to live in the in-law unit while we rented out the main house to tenants who could provide enough in rents to pay our expenses. The numbers really made sense, especially considering that we could live for close to nothing in California. Although it was modestly out of our budget, my wife and I discussed "how can we make this happen?"

We were able to figure it out with the help of family members, and a short time later, we moved into it. For three years, tenants paid rent that helped us pay down our mortgage. When we sold the property, we took our equity from that property and moved it into an apartment complex in Indianapolis.

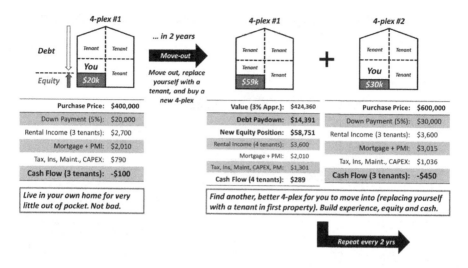

Figure 38

BUY, RENT, REHAB, REFINANCE, REPEAT (BRRRR)

This is an acronym coined by Brandon Turner of Bigger Pockets. To explain this one, we'll have to jump into some math. If you are able to obtain properties cheap enough in a decent area with a good contractor, you can grow your portfolio with *an infinite return*. As long as you can find a property to buy and fix up for around 75% of the final house value (which you won't know until after rehab and a bank goes to appraise it for your loan), you can put your cash seed to work and refinance out your entire original investment. After the smoke clears, you should have a house with a mortgage paid by your tenants. This is the most powerful of the methods. There are ways to do this with no money down using what is referred to as "hard money" but I won't go here due to high risk nature and just not being congruent with a part-time investor. See Figure 39 for a high level view of how this method works. For more details, see the References section on my website for further information. It should be noted this method of investing is the most skill intensive, slow to repeat and requires sizable cash up front, but is also the most lucrative.

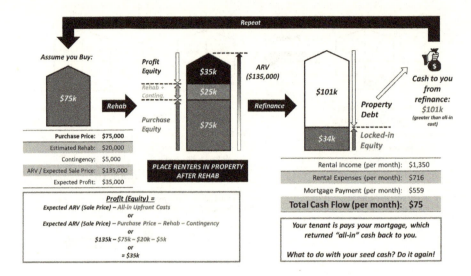

Figure 39

Each of these methods have advantages and disadvantages. As you build your portfolio, the overarching philosophy should be to reinvest your profits so your empire starts to build at a rate where it reinvests on its own. As you grow bigger and bigger, you'll develop processes that work smoother, requiring less time and effort.

In the book "The Richest Man In Babylon" by George S. Klason, Arkad, the protagonist in several of the parables is advised not to eat the fruits of his golden "children" (investments) and instead invest them. This investment advice holds true now, as it did back in the early days of civilization. Why not reinvest your profits into your portfolio until it starts to generate enough profits to run on its own and support you as well?

OVERARCHING SINGLE FAMILY PHILOSOPHY

As a real estate investor who once focused on single-family homes, we highly recommend that you plan to build either a portfolio of single-family homes or none at all. Having income from other properties to help offset any losses or maintenance on other properties is essential for longevity in the space. With one property, if the A/C breaks or the tenant leaves, you have no income to fall back on to offset the loss or mortgage payments and this experience hurts alot when you're putting food on the table with your own income and wanting to spend it out of state on a broken furnace. Building a portfolio of single-family homes allows them to help each other and give you economies of scale in property management expenses, insurance, and maintenance. Understand that when you start out, your goal in the long term should never be a single property, but rather an entire self-sustaining portfolio.

After completing a few properties, it wouldn't hurt to put a business growth plan together to help you reach your financial, or number of properties, goal. Even if you don't have any property, it can help solidify and motivate you to keep investing. We are looking to create a self-standing income machine that has the ability to invest with its own profits. Over time, the cash flow alone, when reinvested, will turn your cash-flow gentle stream into a raging current. The timing is up to you when you are ready to unplug. If this is the hardest decision you have to make in your finances you'll be doing well for yourself.

See Figure 40 for an example of two identical investors who spend $100k on four properties in year one and continue to invest for four years. The difference in results between one who eats the profits of the houses immediately and another who reinvests all of his gains in a ten year period are quite staggering.

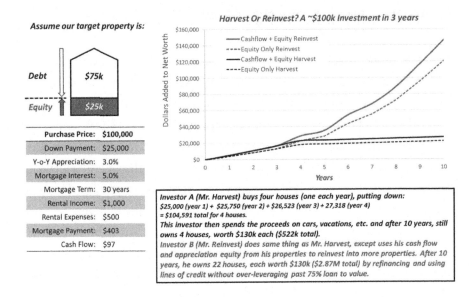

Figure 40

Now that we've explored the single-family route, you should be able to determine which methodology to pursue (turnkey or DIY). You should also have a basic understanding of real estate dynamics and how to talk to people in your market. Yes, this approach involves a lot of work. If this all seems too much, there is another way, which we will discuss in the next chapter. This method is a more passive form of investing that might be right for you at some point in your investing career. That moment may be now. Let's explore this together.

ACTION STEPS

➤ Look back at Figure 32. How many mistakes can you identify in the underwriting for the property on the right on Confusion St., assuming that Wellwritten Ave is in the same city / market?

➤ Select up to three markets to explore and write the name of one of the markets to start your mock underwriting.

➤ What are your key criteria?

My target market(s): _____

My cap rate target is: _____

My purchase price target is: _____

My extra screening criteria is: _____

➤ Underwrite five properties in an area of one of your target markets using your criteria shown above. What was your cash flow on each, assuming a 30 year note at 5% interest? If you need help with underwriting and need a spreadsheet, refer to the tools in Resources section on the website.

CHAPTER 11

LEVERAGING OTHERS FOR PASSIVE MULTIFAMILY SUCCESS

"If you want to go fast, go alone. If you want to go far, go together." —African Proverb

AS SOMEONE JUST starting out in real estate investing, multifamily monetary commitment seems pretty advanced. You may think "Am I ready for something this big?" Don't worry. You'll be leveraging other people's experiences and knowledge to make this happen. But before we get into the in's and out's of this terrific asset class, let's understand why it makes sense to invest in multifamily as opposed to single-family homes. In some cases, it's even better to go directly into multifamily as your first investment.

WHY MULTIFAMILY?

While there are numerous online resources on this subject, here is my take, with a perspective I share as a working full-time professional.

RECESSION-RESISTANT

As of the writing of this book in April 2020, several global economies are showing signs of weakness and economic shock. And as of this writing, COVID-19 has seriously impacted the travel and discretionary spending economies and starting to domino into the entire global economy.[14] However, multifamily has historically been uniquely poised to weather economic storms like the coronavirus. According to research from CBRE, multifamily performed better than any other commercial real estate asset class in both the 2001 recession (only losing 6.7% of rents) and the 2008 recession (in which multifamily lost only 7.9%) as shown in Figure 41. Alternatively, rents recovered faster as well: 10% past the 2001 peaks and 25.7% higher than the 2008 maximum. Most losses in rents came from new construction of high-end multifamily apartments.[15]

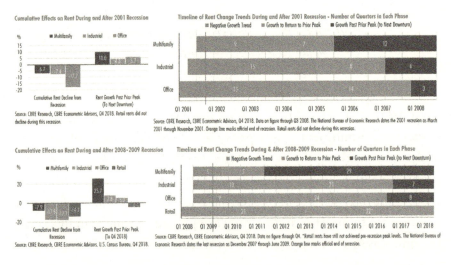

Figure 41

---

14 https://www.grantthornton.com/library/articles/advisory/2020/Economic-Analysis/Economic-Outlook/economic-outlook-march-2020.aspx

15 https://www.cbre.us/research-and-reports/US-Multifamily-Research-Brief-February-2019

This is because shelter is a basic human need, such as food, water and electricity. There will always be a demand for people to reside in a physical space somewhere.

As long as there's a steady increase in population, or net demographic inflow into a market, demand will be there. When we select our apartment buildings to hold and improve, we target C or B class buildings and areas. As investors, our goal is to seek properties that present a high likelihood of improving in the next few years. This can be from either market dynamics alone with upward rent trends and higher demand, but should be coupled with an overall business plan for the building itself.

In targeting B and C class properties, we have a potential demographic to target for people needing to downsize or reduce expenses such as those from A class areas, regardless of where we are in the market cycle. Likewise in good times, we are able to offer a solid B or C product to those moving up from D or C areas with promotions at work or making more money. While lenders like real estate assets such as retail, office and industrial spaces, multifamily is their top choice due to the relative safety multifamily provides in economic conditions throughout the entire market life cycle.

WE ARE A RENTER NATION

As of April 2020, two demographics are shaping the economic landscape to come: Generation Z and aging Millennials (Figure 42).[16] These two age groups are increasing in numbers and will be the focus in the next few decades. Millennials and Gen Z'ers have a higher demand for rentals that offer amenities, proximity to downtown or transit services and walking distance to retail shops. Younger professionals without a family

---

16 https://knoema.com/egyydzc/us-population-by-age-and-generation-in-2020

have a propensity for being mobile with a flexible working arrangement. In addition, their student loan burdens are in excess of $14 trillion, contributing to household shortfalls or prioritization of debt repayment instead of down payments for their own home.

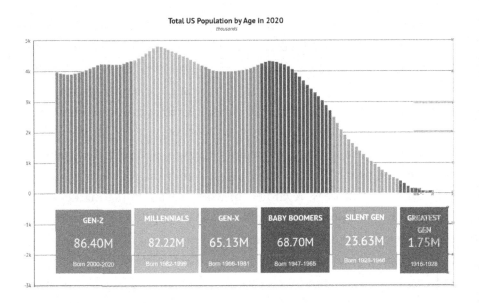

Figure 42

In both cases, the need to be closer to services and the "feel" of luxury living are highly desired and can be provided in multifamily properties. Baby Boomers are also seeking rental units for similar reasons: convenience, services, and a sense of community. Th e number of people renting, either by choice or necessity, remain at healthy levels and show no signs of slowing.

According to FreddieMac and the U.S. Census Bureau, there was a large undersupply of rental units in the late 2010's (Figure 43) and less than one-third of people under 35 own their own home while those 55 and older seem to also be trending downward in homeownership.[17] This is evidence of the growing demand for rental units, even in a healthy economy.

Figure 43

ECONOMIES OF SCALE

In a single-family house, you have one roof, AC, heater, lawn, etc. for a single resident. A single-family portfolio investor would, for example, have 10 roofs, AC's, etc. to maintain rather than just one if all the units were consolidated into a single building. This makes property maintenance easier because getting called one time to replace a roof is much cheaper and efficient than going 10 times to replace each individual roof. Economies of scale also extend to the team you use, including property management and maintenance teams. With properties big enough, you can have a property manager dedicated to just your property and have tighter control on what happens there. Same goes with your maintenance staff and supplies to fix the units. For example, your team can stockpile materials in bulk since all units have similar finishes and upgrades. Other intangibles are also brought to scale, including marketing, insurance and all other expenses on the property.

---

17 https://pretium.com/wp-content/uploads/2019/02/2019-U.S.-Housing-Market-Outlook.pdf

FINANCING AND CONTROL

The financing of multifamily is much different than single-family rentals. While single-family financing is based on the "recently sold" prices, multifamily value is based on NOI you receive and the capitalization rate of the building. This means you have the ability to directly impact the value of the building by changing the bottom line NOI. Remember, the definition of NOI is the result of net building income minus the expenses. So, if you can somehow increase income by raising rents and adding value or decrease expenses such as setting up processes for property management, you are moving the value of your building upwards, often dramatically, due to economies of scale.

COST SEGREGATION

Multifamily has an extra tax advantage over owning a single-family home. It involves our good friend, Depreciation, as Cost Segregation is a method where all of the "materials" used to construct the building is deducted separately as "personal materials" versus a single real estate entity. Your accountant will be able to claim this "accelerated depreciation" for the components that make up the building. Oftentimes this means compressing your depreciation schedule on the value of the entire building from 27.5 years into only 5, 7, or 12 year components depending on the material categories summed up.

This will provide a huge tax boost to you and will show massive "paper losses" to the IRS, since the material in the building is depreciated as personal property and not real property. If done correctly in tax planning and 1031 exchanges, you may never have to pay these taxes. There are depreciation recaptures that have to be paid back, but this calculation is dependent on your personal return and tax situation. As stated before, seek the advice of a tax professional on this to learn more.

HOW APARTMENT / COMMERCIAL BUILDINGS ARE VALUED

Before we go further into the world of multifamily buildings, and your options to invest in them, it's important to understand how their value is determined. Single-family houses are fairly straightforward and most people understand them. But, apartment buildings are valued differently. If two apartment complexes stood side by side on a block, one being 12 units and the other 100 units, how do you determine the value? Surely they must have significantly different values if an investor wanted to buy either.

As we discussed previously, when you cross the threshold of commercial property the values are based on the Net Operating Income of the investment. Remember this term from Chapter 8? Consider the simple relationship below (and as shown in Figure 44) that defines the value of apartment buildings:

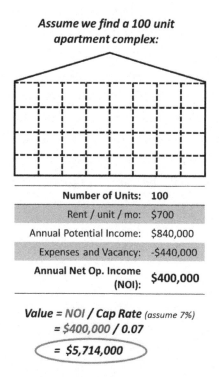

Figure 44

Value of Building (Fair Market Sales Price) = NOI / Cap-Rate

So, the value of the building is based on a combination of NOI (income and expenses) and the market's cap-rate for the area. We discussed how cap-rate determines the market dynamics. In addition to the cap rate for the market and the area, there is also a cap-rate for the building. If it's distressed, the building's cap-rate will be slightly higher than the average cap-rate of the market for this property class, which means the price will be lower. You can use the market's average cap-rate as a starting point, but understand that the building itself will also determine the cap-rate for the purchase. It can vary wildly as well, so getting a grip on valuation and running sample numbers yourself can be helpful.

Compared to single-family housing, investors have much more control over multifamily housing valuation due to Net Operating Income being directly tied to value. For example, if you are able to either increase rents, decrease expenses or vacancies, or even decrease (compress) cap-rates by improving the area around the property or making amenity improvements and increasing offerings to tenants, you can directly and dramatically increase the building's value.

See Figure 45 for an example of how this can be done and how dramati-cally a modest increase in rental income (and, in turn, NOI) can affect building value. Once the building has increased its value, lenders will be happy to write new loans based on that valuation change. The other part of the equation to consider is the cap-rate of the building, dependent on the market cycle, submarket expectations, building condition, location and economic potential. When you implement a business plan and any of those variables change, your cap-rate will also change, meaning your building value will also change. This is why it is important to recognize timing for market cycle cap-rate effect and multifamily experience (for the business plan and market knowledge) to be able to sell the same property for a fair price at lower cap-rates.

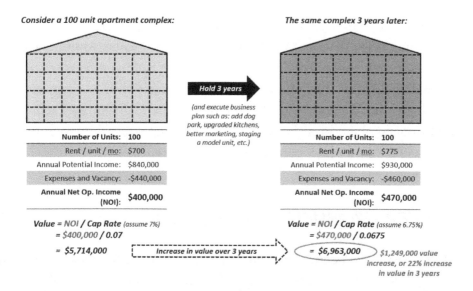

Figure 45

TYPES AND OWNERSHIP

There are several types of multifamily and ownership structures to cover before getting into the meat of what part-time investors should be actively seeking. For completeness, multifamily buildings can be held by individuals (otherwise known as sole proprietorships), partnerships, trusts, corporations, and potentially any mix of those. Multifamily also comes in two types, residential and commercial. If a property is meant for residential use and is four units or less, then the same rules for single-family houses apply on the lending and valuation side. In that case, they can be private residences with low money down, and the value of the property from appraisals is based on recently sold properties nearby. If five units or more, it is considered commercial and the lending requirements and property valuation determination change. You can't just use comps such as a fourplex, triplex or duplex in these situations. Generally, if there is a lender involved at this point, they will require title be held in an LLC or corporate structure.

However, I don't generally recommend part-time investors take something larger than four units down in their own name, without help or at least some experience. It can be a frustrating endeavor to get started in multifamily this way, unless you are comfortable with low cap-rates and high risk. We don't want frustration because it discourages action and progress. Let's move on to the most natural ownership type and structure meant for busy part-time real estate professionals.

MULTIFAMILY SYNDICATIONS

We've arrived at the most natural fit for most real estate investors who have a full-time job and little time. Although the word syndication is a complicated one, don't let it intimidate you. It simply means "pooling funds together and executing as a group."

In a syndication, there are two types of investors. These are the limited partners and general partners. Limited partners (LP) are cash investors like yourself seeking a return while general partners (GP) are the people with the skills, connections and experience needed to make the investment run successfully. The limited partners, once identified and committed, contribute cash to the syndication and, depending on the amount needed for down payment, closing costs, and construction funds, will receive an equity piece in proportion to the amount needed. See Figure 46 for an overview of the general syndication structure. Remember since leverage will be placed on the property, any contribution will be magnified by 2, 3 or even 4 times to match the value of the building.

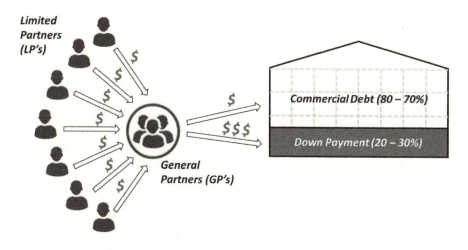

Figure 46

In order to invest in multifamily properties or syndications, all individuals participating must be either an accredited investor or a sophisticated investor. There are some managers who have a specific syndication model for accredited investors only. An accredited investor is someone with either:

- a high net worth (around $1M without primary residence) and/or
- high income (around the $200,000 income mark for single individuals and $300,000 for married households).

The Securities and Exchange Commission (SEC) views these people as qualified enough to take financial risks.

A sophisticated investor, on the other hand, is someone with a relationship with the management team and understands the risks involved with the investment. The syndication management team must do significant due diligence in the relationship to ensure they are a "suitable" investor and understand the risks involved in this type of investment.

The process starts with the general partners putting information about the property, the business plan and projections for qualified limited partners (LPs). Any questions the LP's have, must and should be answered by the GP's. It should be noted that syndication structures are heavily monitored by the Securities And Exchange Commission (SEC) due to past abuse of the syndication structure by some bad apples. Experienced syndicator GP's know what is going to be asked, have lawyers help draft agreements and advise all LP's and GP's on any questions if needed.

One thing to know about syndications is the exact details of how funds contributed from LP's and GP's are translated into equity. While it's true funds invested by an LP do convert into equity of the property, GP's are rewarded by receiving both walk-in-equity due to their willingness and experience from operating and putting the investment together.

When times are good and prices are low, some GP's will take up to 40% of the entire equity on the building, and the LP's will contribute all the cash and receive the remaining 60% equity. Even with that 60% equity, the LP's will be well taken care of and should still make decent cash-on-cash returns that rival or beat the stock market and offer fantastic tax benefits. When times are a bit more tight, GP's may only take 20% while LP's have the remaining 80% in order to make the cash-on-cash returns in line with LP expectations (around 8%–11% per annum).

Make sure you also review and understand the offering material well. Ask the management team lots of questions if you need to. Good operators welcome thoughtful questions and love to share knowledge. As with single-family property, after your first few, you will get the hang of it and it will become second nature. See Figure 47 to see an example of how contribution funds are actually used at closing and how it relates to your equity in the property as an LP, assuming an 80%–20% split.

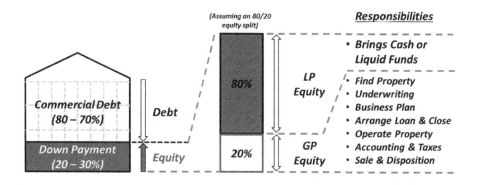

Figure 47

Once you've joined the investment, the process as a whole works as shown in Figure 48:

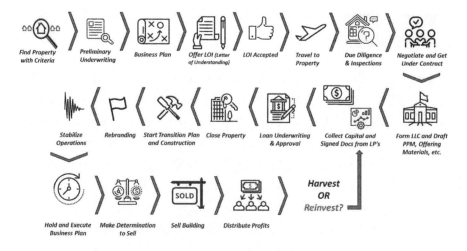

Figure 48

This is the standard process by which syndications are run. Some variations and sequencing may vary from each multifamily operator. It's time-consuming on the front end to put together when starting out as a GP, rife with legal paperwork, marketing preparation and due diligence that often involves frequent travel to the property.

Obviously, as a part-time investor, this is looking like a full-time job to do everything yourself. But only if you are the GP operator. If you are an LP, your job is to vet the operator to make sure they are legitimate and sincere, understand the market well and property itself, its risks, and its business plan, sign documentation and contribute capital to the property.

RETURNS AND MEASURES OF SUCCESS

After submitting capital for your equity stake into the building, you have become a real estate investor. What happens next is why you invested in the first place. You will be receiving returns from the property in the same five ways as mentioned in Chapter 2. This is a wonderful opportunity to learn more about investing from some of the best players in the industry (multifamily operators) as well.

- *Cash flow.* This is the profit received from rents distributed to all the investors from the operations of the apartment building. If the building receives $50,000 per month in income, has $25,000 in expenses and $15,000 in financing costs, the net cash flow from the building, ($10,000 / month) is split among all the LP investors according to their equity ownership.
- *Depreciation.* Each year, as an LP, you will receive a K-1 from the GP's that spells out the performance of the property in proportion to your equity stake. Due to cost segregation advantages in larger multifamily properties, you will most likely be showing a "paper loss" on the property despite the otherwise taxable income received from cash-flow distributions. While you and your coworkers in the office may earn a similar salary, you'll have a huge discount on your tax bill because these "losses" will offset your taxable income from your W-2 or your total taxable income on your 1099. There are some exceptions to this, including if your adjustable gross income is above a certain

threshold in the $150,000 range, in which those losses will carry over into future years until you qualify to take them. Again, consult your tax professional on this.

- *Appreciation / Sale / Liquidation.* Obviously, when the property is sold according to the business plan, you will receive your part of the sale price in proportion to the equity you own. If the GP's have done their job right, you should receive your original capital and then some. Oftentimes, very successful syndications can return 1 ½ to 3 times the original investment at resale. While capital gains and depreciation recapture would normally apply here, you can elect to do a 1031 exchange and defer those taxes. You'd defer all of your gains by exchanging your equity funds into another property (or two) which further magnifies your tax benefits and cash flow on future investments.
- *Debt paydown.* Same as single-family property, we will have fixed debt on the property that will be paid down by our tenants and returned to us with the sale of the property.
- *Equity capture.* While this effect may be there, it is not felt much due to the fact we are buying from a much more sophisticated person, an investor, and not a homeowner. There is potential for you to purchase apartment buildings cheaply which is expressed as a risk premium, but this method of making money is not as lucrative as with single-family or small apartments. The skill, relationships and experience level of the GP operators determine the actual benefit value here from acquisition.

While all this is great, how will we gauge the success of our investment? We can list the sources of these returns and income streams, but how do they compare to other vehicles or even other similar syndications? The major ways to evaluate performance on the property are cash-on-cash (similar to what we discussed in Chapter 8) and internal rate of return (IRR).

CASH-ON-CASH

This is exactly how you imagine it. For example, placing $100,000 as an LP into a syndication in cash, might net you $600 / month in income, in which case you'd have a cash-on-cash (dollar for dollar) annual return of ($600 x 12 / $100,000) = 7.2%. This is the simplest way to express performance during the hold period. You'll also get tax benefits, but since this is personal for each individual, the GP's cannot estimate this for you. A good syndication can offer C-o-C returns above 7% in tight times and markets, and up to 10–12% or greater in good times and hot markets.

INTERNAL RATE OF RETURN

This is the actual return on your investment that considers both cash flow and sale / liquidation income from the investment. Obviously, you won't know what this is until the property is sold and your investment is returned, but the GP's usually set a target for IRR and try to hit this to determine sale timing. IRR is a true measure of the property's combined cash flows plus the large payout at sale. It takes into account the time value of money. You can think of this as determining what your cash flow would be each year if you somehow were able to see the future, and spread the sale profits into each year in addition to the cash flow, considering inflation over a 3–5 year hold. See Figure 49 for a visual explanation of how IRR works in two scenarios—a 3 year hold with modest increases in cash flow versus a 5 year hold.

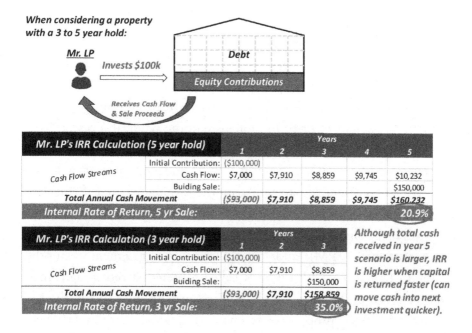

Figure 49

Internal rates of returns are calculated with the time value of money in mind. Even though they are hard to visualize without using a calculator, IRR should be considered alongside Cash-on-Cash return metrics in measure of performance. It is a uniform figure that can be used to capture how much cash you've received over the life of the investment including the sale of the property and how quickly you are making returns. This figure can be calculated using spreadsheets and long formulas that I won't get into here, but you can find resources online and on our website.

One downside to investing in multifamily syndications is your cash is tied up in the investment for 3–5 years or more. You've lost direct control of the cash you've invested, but in the case of foul play, the SEC will have your back. This is why all syndications are governed strictly and highly regulated. Another downside is that inexperienced or undercapitalized syndicators may do what is called a "cash call" in which they require investors to contribute additional money into the investment to resolve a construction issue, vacancy or property management conflict, property tax problem, or so on. The best general partners and investors will never actually ask investors for more funds. Truly dedicated operators would rather lose their own cash since this causes mistrust along with resentment and reflects poorly on the professionalism of the syndicator operator.

To mitigate risk on your end, great GP's include an option to sell your equity stake to a general partner or another limited partner if you wish. These rules are outlined in the paperwork distributed to investors when they originally sign up for the investment called the "Private Placement Memorandum" (PPM) and the "Operating Agreement." Another method of preserving LP safety is called a preferred return agreement (outlined in the PPM), in which the managers promise to pay the LP's *first* from the excess property cash flow, and the *remainder* flows to them. For example, if an investment is providing a 7% preferred return ("pref") and the property only makes 6% on the bottom line, the general partner's portion of the cash flow from their 20%–40% equity stake is sacrificed to cover the LP's until their 7% "pref" cash-on-cash return is met. In cases where the cash flow is significantly lower, around 4%, the "pref" will continue to accrue throughout pay periods. Then, when cash flows recover, the GP's are caught up to the 7% until both GP's and LP's have received income in line with their equity.

As an LP, understand you'll get all the benefits of owning real estate without having the hassle of dealing with agents, property managers, etc. We let our largest asset, our earning income, go to work for us by converting those funds into equity via the easiest and most scalable way possible: by leveraging someone else's experience. While you'd be forfeiting some control on your money for the next 3–5 years you could otherwise have in building a single-family portfolio yourself, this method allows equity to build while freeing up time needed to maintain relationships with family, friends and work.

With passive real estate investing as a limited partner, you truly do get all of the benefits of real estate investing with minimal efforts. Being in a full-time job, your unfair advantage is your salary. Using this to efficiently obtain equity in high performing properties as an LP is a strong play.

Refer to the example in Figure 50 to see how a successful multifamily syndication looks from the LP point of view. While there are many different ways a syndication can generate profits, the Figure below is one way to achieve the returns a limited partner expects.

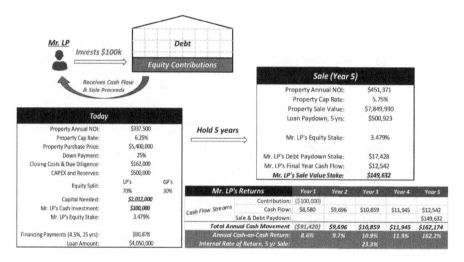

Figure 50

SELECTING A GOOD SYNDICATION ACQUISITION & MANAGEMENT TEAM

While the previous discussion has helped outline the overall approach of apartment buildings and how the process works, this should only be your educational starting point. Repetition is king when it comes to new knowledge and habits, and you will want a syndication team that above all helps educate you every step of the way. By now you should be comfortable with a basic understanding of what to expect in an apartment investment. Now what?

By far, the most important success factor in an apartment investment is the team who will manage the investment. Once the team is aligned on what improvements will be brought to the building (along with a willingness to implement them), that translates to efficient operations and high returns, while providing a smooth experience with full transparency. The following should be considered when looking for a good syndication operator to start your journey in multifamily investing as an LP.

HOW DID YOU FIND THEM?

When looking for an investment, did you Google and pick the first one you saw? Did you find them on a webinar? Or did you get to know them by a referral from someone you trust and had already invested with them? These questions make a big difference and can give you an idea how much thought was put into you selecting this team. If you ran into them by happen-chance … Well, would you trust a significant amount of your savings to someone you barely know anything about?

HOW DO THEY COMMUNICATE?

When you first encounter these individuals or their representatives, how professional are they? Do you get a feeling for how trustworthy they are? What does your gut tell you about these folks? Remember you will be working and doing business with them for at least 3–5 years on one property. That's a long time. How often do they communicate and are they happy to see you? Do they show you common courtesy? Are they compatible with your personality? These are important to consider in building trust for a business relationship that has the potential to last a long time.

WHAT IS THEIR TRACK RECORD?

What properties have they already closed on and what is their track record in multiple apartment complexes? Who are they working with and how experienced are they? How motivated are they to see you succeed and how seriously do they treat their previous investments?

MARKETING MATERIAL?

Similar to the question how they communicate, but what does their material look like? Does it appear like a well-polished machine, focused on the details and great work down to the granular level on everything they do? Is the marketing material non-existant or look like it has been piecemealed together in a quick and shoddy fashion? Since marketing material these teams put together should represent them in the very best light, how does that look? Is there a general awareness of service and mindfulness of the investor / customer?

VERTICAL INTEGRATION?

The most successful and well-established multifamily investors have hired their own property management staff and maintenance teams directly on payroll. These players run the tightest ships since they have control of their property down to every last detail. They don't rely on third-party property management like most teams do, which can be expensive and inefficient if not done correctly. It may even affect returns as they get adjusted to the property itself.

These are important things to consider when looking for someone to assist you in your investing goals. Now that we've covered the fundamentals, we turn to focus on you. What can we do to boost your investing game or get it started? Let's get your plan in gear.

ACTION STEPS

- Go to LoopNet.com and search for multifamily properties in your market. Usually properties with higher unit counts and higher values have better information about the financials of the building and the surrounding areas.
- For one property, try to calculate the property cap-rate (or verifying the cap-rate they have listed) by using their asking price and the NOI reported.
- Read through any brochures, offering memorandums, or anything else available for the properties that came up in your search. Note the differences in the listing quality and information available. Try to identify a few places where listing brokers or sellers could "fudge" numbers and boost their NOI.
- For one property where unit rent information is available, compare the "market rent" to the actual rents being asked. Use Apartments.com or other resources to determine what the Seller is advertising their rents for.

Bed / Baths Size	LoopNet (market rents)	Apartments.com (current rents)
_ bed / _ bath: ____ ft2	$_____ / mo	$_____ / mo
_ bed / _ bath: ____ ft2	$_____ / mo	$_____ / mo
_ bed / _ bath: ____ ft2	$_____ / mo	$_____ / mo

How does accounting for market rents affect NOI and what you'd need to pay as a potential buyer?
_____
_____

- Find a webinar on Meetup.com or on Google to get a feel for some of the operators out there offering investment opportunities.

CHAPTER 12

YOUR TURN... THE NEXT STEPS

"Do you want to know who you are? Don't ask. Act! Action will delineate and define you." —Thomas Jefferson

MULTIFAMILY INVESTING IS a powerful, hands-off method to get started and build serious wealth on the side while in your professional career. If done correctly it can grow so quickly your LEGO block empire will generate more safety and freedom than your full-time job. It is a mechanism to give you tax advantages along with experience in business and entrepreneurialism. It truly is the ideal passive investment.

However, if you are more hands-on and don't mind the ups and downs of owning your own business and managing people while directing your destiny, starting with a single-family and moving up to apartment complexes could be right for you. While you can also start with apartment complexes, some professionals don't recommend this as a part-time investor. The process could be too overwhelming unless you have considerable flexibility in your job and time.

DECISION TIME

So what will you do? Which route resonates with you the most? I really want you to think about this, because in the coming pages, we're setting goals and putting an action plan together for you at a high level. Take a minute to stop, reflect, consider your options and what's best for your monetary future.

At this point, you've either made your decision, or remain unsure about the next step. Use the flowchart in Figure 51 to help inform yourself towards your decision. No matter which way you've picked, it is now time to execute and put a plan in place.

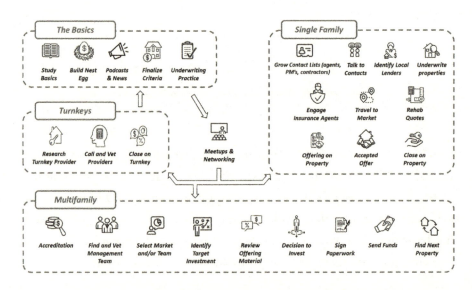

Figure 51

If you decided on the single-family path, I have an outline of activities that allowed me to reach my goals, then began working towards multifamily investing as a general partner. Consider these activities I went through as a part-time investor that led me to my first rental properties (see Figure 36 in Chapter 10 for how long it took me).

- Self-Study on Basics
- Save up Cash
- Networking
- Evaluate / Determine Criteria
- Contacted Wholesalers
- Trip Out to Market
- Meet Property Managers & Contacts
- Call Recommended Contacts
- Property Underwriting
- Get Property Under Contract
- Close Property
- Start Rehab or Cleanup
- Marketing Begins
- Tenant Moves In
- Rental Income Arrives & Stabilization

Using this list as a guide of activities you will need to tackle to reach your goal of owning your first rental property, modify the list so it makes the most sense to you. Write all these down on a sheet of paper out by hand. This is your action plan. Build your action plan in chronological order, starting from the top and going down to the bottom with the end result being your annual goal. Leave room to the far right as shown.

Now, with those activities and the end goal at the bottom, assign a timeframe to each activity, keeping in mind you can only divide your time so it covers one year, because by then, you'll need to accomplish your goal.

A word of caution here: when I started out, I didn't build a plan. Instead, I spent lots of time reading and researching and then just bought the first couple of properties that came across my desk that "made sense." What I didn't know at the time was that I was only looking at the attractive numbers on the property and was too loose in my underwriting. This house was only $18,000. What could go wrong at that price? I was about $5,000 into the rehab when I found out that my contractor was not moving forward with work because of a bedbug infestation hidden in some junk stored in the basement. I took all of this, including the inspection report, to a mentor who then advised me to "run as far as I can" from this property. I proceeded to do this, but ended up losing around $10,000 in sunk rehab and lower resale–all because I didn't have a plan to follow. I let impatience get the best of me and it cost me a significant amount of cash. Don't be this person.

WHAT DOES SUCCESS LOOK LIKE FOR YOU?

In order to provide motivation and help plan out your long-term goal and how you'll get there, let's go ahead and build out a financial plan to amass your LEGO blocks that extends past one year. The route you take depends on whether or not you decide to go the single-family or multifamily route. Funding your start also depends on which "seeds" you'd like to use to move forward. Remember that investing only works really well when you are diversified, even in your real estate holdings. If you aren't going to commit to building up a portfolio over time, I'd ask you to strongly consider not investing at all.

Back in Chapter 10, we saw the powerful differences in results of Mr. Harvest versus Mr. Reinvest. What we'd like to do is build out a model for you to follow, whether you have decided to do single-family or multifamily portfolio building. I've created a high level spreadsheet for you to play with to see what happens if you reinvest your capital funds back into rental property or multifamily equity over time.

If you'd like to do this on your own, or play with the sheet yourself, head over to the Premium Resources section at the link below to download your sheet and see what happens if you follow your blueprint to build your empire.

Link: http://elevateequity.org/the-book/book-resources-the-premium-section/
Password: IAmReadyToAct2020

We covered a tremendous amount of material and I know it's a lot to digest. Regardless of where you are in your journey, we hope this has been useful and you've enjoyed the ride. I'm excited for those who are starting out and found inspiration from anything you found in this book. Real estate investing can seem intimidating and complex, but when you break it down, it's really a simple process. Do not, however, confuse simple with easy. We encourage you to stick with it and let time work for you. This will not get you rich overnight, but will certainly put you on that path and allow you to keep more of what you make.

In the end, it all comes down to you. This method of slowly obtaining cash flowing and appreciating real estate is one of the many ways to eventually create your own financial independence through real estate investing. At the very least, I hope I've made you think about your future, which alone is very exciting.

I'm humbled and thankful you've taken the time to learn real estate investing from me. I was in your shoes a few short years ago and it's been quite a journey to get where I am now. If I was able to teach you at least one thing, even if part-time real estate investing is not for you, I am happy I've done my job. I wish you all the success in the future and hope your dreams come true.

Remember to embrace discipline and you'll have all the freedom you've ever dreamed of.

We are here for you if you need support and are always developing resources for full-time professionals to invest in real estate. Reach out to us online to learn more. There, you can sign up for courses that can help walk you through the content in the book and really get you started.

Best wishes to you and your journey, wherever it may lead you!

ACTION STEPS

➤ What is your main goal to accomplish one year from now?

_____

_____

_____

➤ What actions can be taken to get closer to your goal?

_____

_____

_____

➤ Why is this important to you? Who will benefit and what will the benefit be?

_____

_____

_____

➤ After completing this book in its entirety, what one thing will you do RIGHT NOW to make the effort spent in reading this book USEFUL to you?

_____

_____

_____

ABOUT THE AUTHOR

DEREK CLIFFORD IS a successful real estate investor of single and multifamily properties, acquiring 13 units out-of-state while in his first year of acquisitions while working a full time job. He is also the founder and CEO of Elevate Equity, a firm that partners with individuals and companies to purchase, improve, and operate cash flowing multifamily apartment real estate. He also loves to give back his knowledge and has a passion for breaking down complex topics into easy to explain topics. He's helped many people start, maintain, and grow their portfolios to achieve their own financial independence.

You can contact him directly at derek@elevateequity.org
or visit his website at http://elevateequity.org/

CAN YOU HELP?

Thank You For Reading My Book!

I really appreciate all of your feedback, and I love hearing what you have to say.

I need your input to make the next version of this book and my future books better.

Please leave me an honest review on Amazon letting me know what you thought of the book.

Thanks so much!

NOW IT'S YOUR TURN

Discover the EXACT three-step blueprint you need to become a bestselling author in as little as three months.

Self-Publishing School helped me, and now I want them to help you with this FREE resource to begin outlining your book!

Even if you're busy, bad at writing, or don't know where to start, you CAN write a bestseller and build your best life.

With tools and experience across a variety of niches and professions, Self-Publishing School is the only resource you need to take your book to the finish line!

DON'T WAIT

Say "YES" to becoming a bestseller:
https://self-publishingschool.com/friend/

Follow the steps on the page for a FREE resource to get started on your book and unlock a discount to get started with Self-Publishing School

Made in the USA
Monee, IL
25 August 2020